THROUGH THE CABIN DOOR

Praise for THROUGH THE CABIN DOOR

"Richard Carter's strikingly poetical essay collection, THROUGH THE CABIN DOOR, reads easy and reads calm, like its prequel, CABIN FEVER. Through his gentle, passionate and deeply personal examinations of humanity's proper relationship with wild nature, the author shares universal truths with readers far beyond his Lake Michigan environs. Carolyn Kenney-Carter's rich and poignant pencil drawings flow in perfect harmony with her husband's words."

> — David Petersen, naturalist, teacher and author of *On the Wild Edge: In Search of a Natural Life*

"This book is like those tiny, erratic vole tunnels beneath the snow. It lets the reader enter a deeper world of nature that makes the concerns of day-to-day life seem petty. Sample THROUGH THE CABIN DOOR. Take it home. Light a bayberry candle, and marvel as osprey, chipmunks, rabbits, as well as songbirds, woodpeckers, owls, hawks and waves of wildflower blossoms come alive. The drawings of Carolyn Kenney-Carter, Richard Carter's artist/wife, are charming and beautifully invite readers into his world. You will cherish this Wisconsin literary treasure the rest of your life."

> — John Lehman, founder of *Rosebud Magazine* and literary editor of *Wisconsin People and Ideas*

"These pages are imbued with a deep sense of place, profound and stilled time. They bear witness faithfully and powerfully to this beautiful and fragile world."

> — Bill McKibben, author of *The End of Nature* and *Enough: Staying Human in an Engineered World*

"Richard Carter brings one THROUGH THE CABIN DOOR into a realm of treasures of the past and encounters with trees and other beings. Each essay is a lesson to be learned, raising the need to get out and explore the world and let nature speak to us. Like John Muir, he has known deep connections and is able to bring readers to a greater awareness of the earth."

> — Marion Moran, Wisconsin interpretive naturalist and humanitarian

"The joy of reading Richard Carter's essays is that they lead you, step by step, to a deep and true connection with the natural world. You fall in love with the proud mama turkey as she struts to protect her brood. You ski into the woods along with Carter, pause with him and turn your cold face to the warm sun. You feel, maybe for the first time in your life, the layers of the Silurian Sea beneath your feet. And in that split second, you realize that your life will never be the same."

> — Judy Bridges, founder, Redbird Studio writing center and author of *Shut Up and Write*

THROUGH THE CABIN DOOR

ESSAYS BY
RICHARD E. CARTER

DRAWINGS BY
CAROLYN KENNEY-CARTER

C. Kenney-Carter

First Edition, First Printing 2011

Library of Congress Cataloging-in-Publication Data

Carter, Richard E.
      Through the cabin door / essays by Richard E. Carter ;
      drawings by Carolyn Kenney-Carter. — 1st ed.

      p. : ill. ; cm.

      ISBN: 978-0-9846433-0-1

      1. Natural history—Wisconsin—Door County. 2. Door County
      (Wis.) 3. Nature. I. Kenney-Carter, Carolyn. II. Title.

QH105.W6 C37 2011
508.775/63   2011906322

Appleport Press
2408 North 73rd Street
Wauwatosa, WI 53213-1212

To share the journey to true connection
with the natural world and its creatures,
with each other and with ourselves

— R.E.C. and C.K.-C.

contents

C. Kenney-Carter ©

acknowledgments

Whenever I think of gratitude, I cannot help but return to memories of those persons who had such a profound influence on me decades ago when the writer in me was first trying to get up off all fours, to walk, talk, and write like one. Marcie Telander, the mistress of story, drew me out past the creaking hinges of my shuttered creativity into the blinking light with her enthusiasm, support, and compassion. It was though she had touched me on the shoulder with a magic wand and commanded me to live. Then Norb Blei's tough disciplinary lessons about showing up to write regardless of your circumstances taught me I could do far more than I imagined. I learned to scorn the idle foolishness of sitting around waiting for the muse to rouse, and to "just do it." Eloise Fink and Sue Brabant taught me how to ride the wild pony of poetry with more form and grace than merely clinging to its mane in hope we might both survive the ride.

In more recent years, as *Through the Cabin Door* began to emerge, essay by essay, Judy Bridges and my fellow writers at her Redbird Studios in Milwaukee walked every step with me. Judy's take-no-prisoners approach to weak writing or inappropriate words helped keep me honest and honed my own editorial skills. I also received solid supportive critiques from my fellow writers at the Appleton chapter of the Wisconsin Regional Writers' Association during my years in Oshkosh.

Most of all, I want to express my gratitude to Carolyn Kenney-Carter, my wife and partner in this creative adventure. Not only has she added her own expression of these magical places through her artwork which graces this volume, she has supported me through periods of doubt and been my ally in the cause of nature so vital to both of us. Nothing is like having someone who understands what you are trying to articulate as a person who has the intimate knowledge of nature herself. Her editorial comments have often brought clarity to a muddied passage, filled in gaps and pointed out areas I needed to address in more depth. While I have often referred to her as the "Queen of Commas," her editorial expertise has been invaluable.

Philosophically, I am deeply indebted to two giants in their fields, Jens Jensen, the father of the school of natural landscaping in America, and perhaps our wisest and most articulate environmentalist, Aldo Leopold. Their viewpoints and ethics have permeated my thinking and changed me at depth.

— *Richard E. Carter*

Since the publication and reprinting of our first book, *Cabin Fever*, I have been most thankful for two things in my life and my work. These are the inspiration of the natural world and its creatures, and Richard Carter's insights and experiences, as reflected in his new essays. As my husband and creative partner, Richard has given me vivid images and engaging writing to respond to on paper, and that team effort has been most meaningful and satisfying. He has shared in both the challenges and the successes of this project, and been generous in his praise and enthusiasm for the drawings in this book.

My personal connection with nature has likewise illuminated my way. This happens not just with grand, dramatic venues, but with more common places and spaces and subtle, intimate details that the busy world often rushes past and does not truly see. It might be a twisted cedar, clinging to a rocky ledge; a small flock of Canada geese, coming in to land; a clump of spring bloodroot, blooming behind a tree stump; a tiny eastern gray tree frog, perched on a chunk of dolomite—all the work of the Great Creator.

I am also deeply grateful to the instructors and workshop leaders whose focused critical comment on my work has helped me to develop as an artist in recent years. Special thanks to Jean Crane, Ellen Fountain, Adele Earnshaw and Joe Garcia, Barbara Farrell and Betty Delinck.

— *Carolyn Kenney-Carter*

C. Kenney-Carter ©

introduction

When I finished my first book of essays, *Cabin Fever*, in 1995, I didn't anticipate doing a sequel like *Through the Cabin Door*. I intended to pursue writing interests in poetry, animal stories, aviation and other non-fiction subjects. These topics did find their voices; however, nature and Door County were not through with me. Their epiphanies kept popping up like targets in a shooting gallery, and would not be ignored. So, I surrendered. I didn't plan or outline *Through the Cabin Door* in advance. Instead, the topics selected me, and I served them. So now, having finished the last of these essays, I look back to see where I have come from and where I have been led.

For me, writing a nature essay is something like going fishing. Thinking of "going writing," my attention may first be drawn by a curious glint, a "lure" in my tackle box. It could be the sparkle of an image or a hint of promise, saying, "Pick me." Then, I cast it out into the vast, deep, calm waters of Universal Mind. I play the line, become fully absorbed in the action, imagining the line connected to my mind. With patience, movement and cooperation with something unseen, the tug of excitement announces I have connection with something deep beyond my immediate knowing. Now, playing the line becomes more intense. With a bit of skill or maybe a dash of luck, eventually I land the beauty I've been seeking.

Skiing winter woodland trails can be more than mere exercise when I allow myself to be really present to the small details around me. A light dusting of tawny seed chaff on pure, crystal snow at the base of a dried wildflower, announces a deer mouse below the surface. Tiny, erratic mounds reveal vole tunnels beneath the snow, and take me deeper into the forgotten world of nature. So much more life all around me, it takes me out of my petty concerns, and into the real world. I become absorbed in the scenes about me, the questions they raise. The enchantment of seeing more and more clearly grows, as with progressively sharper lenses, until I start to feel the connection, a belonging to something greater.

Wallace Stegner calls this profound link with nature "having a sense of place." For me, that includes more than the obvious familiar landmarks, vistas, climate, and the like. It goes beyond the whole kettle of memories associated with a locale and takes you to something more intense, a vibrational field, where you feel you are part of it All. You are woven into the fabric of what is present at the heart level, not just a casual observer.

Here, you resonate with all of nature and not just with man's shaping of the land. You feel you belong here. You want to know more and more about the history, the land, its creatures, plant life, rhythms, and how you fit in. You move past the diversions of entertainment, seasonal fairs, and endless shops into the forgotten heart of nature to touch its pulse and choose to vibrate with it while you can, knowing you can't pack it up with you when you leave.

To achieve this, you must be willing to step beyond casual, superficial observations and allow yourself to sink into the land, sky, forests, meadows, and waters and let nature speak to you. This may take some time and practice, because most of us have forgotten this precious connection and separated ourselves from nature, but the journey to reconnection is worth the effort.

Aldo Leopold's wise observation, "There are those who can exist without wilderness and those who cannot," contains a great deal of sad truth, but I have a slightly different take on it. I see a great middle area between the two poles on wilderness, where there are those who have merely forgotten early childhood experiences with nature and those who have been deprived of them. I like to believe that all of us may be like the seed banks of wildflowers in a degraded prairie. All we need to respond is to have the alien plants cleared from our fertile soil, for the light to shine upon us again, and we will bloom.

I offer my own experience as an example. As a little boy, I went to visit my grandmother in a tiny town on the Ohio River each summer. I discovered nature for the first time in the hills and valleys surrounding a town that lived off the river. I had high bluffs to climb, unfenced forests to explore, snakes and frogs to catch, river mud to ooze between my toes, and strong currents to push against my shins. Nothing like it existed in my bland, flat, homogenous, suburban hometown, only vacant subdivided lots waiting for the Depression to end. Later, as an older child, I could make the 12 miles on my bike to vast forest preserves following the Des Plaines River and explore.

When I became a young man, college and the demands of a new career took me in a totally different direction. I became an urban planner, thoroughly captivated by the charms and excitements of city life. I thought I had left my love affair with nature behind along with other "childish" pursuits. Yet, in mid-life, when the stress of urban living and working began to leave me spent and discontent, I began to find myself being drawn to the woods on Sundays without really knowing why. All I knew was that with each step into the woods, I became lighter, more peaceful. I wanted to know more and more about how such a magical healing happened.

Looking back on the beginning of this quest, I can see how I was led in making a life-changing decision to take a deceptively innocuous nature study course at The Clearing in Ellison Bay, Wisconsin. My dormant seeds exploded in wild enthusiasms of YES! I had been presented with the key to the passageway I had been seeking. Now, thirty years later, I can look back on a path that was meant to be. The philosophy of The Clearing's founder, Jens Jensen, about the use of natural, native landscaping and how man's well-being depended upon retaining a connection with nature, resonated deeply with me. Although I never met the man, I felt as though he knew me, knew what this harried urbanite needed.

The potpourri of essays in *Through the Cabin Door* is my invitation to you to accompany me on a personal journey into the heart of nature – settings, encounters, and experiences. I hope you might see what I have seen, even feel what I have felt, but mostly I want to encourage you to reflect on nature in your own surroundings in new ways. My ambition is to awaken what has slept in all of us too long, to help set aside old, rigid judgments and ways of looking at the world around us. Let us simply look with the eyes of an innocent child of wonder and exclaim, "Wow! What about that?"

through the cabin door

*T*urning south off Appleport Lane,
through a brief breach in tall cedar,
and hedge of thimbleberry,
twisting the ignition, hand paused
on the latch, I take two cleansing breaths,
step out on needle-softened earth,
and slam the door on a life now history.

I stand in a cone of silence,
its sounds too fine for my coarse
urban ears to detect.
Pungent balsam fir extends
welcoming boughs, and the musk
of deepening decay floats up
from each easy footstep.
The wind rattles bare poplar arms.

My path leads past the brown gingerbread
cottage, its shutters, picket fence flower boxes,
and scroll board decorated with white icing,
a civilized face presented to
the passing world.
Beyond, it narrows to the width of a single foot,
dips into an icy swale still in the
shin-numbing chill of spring melt water,
a small toll extracted to enter the real woods.

Shiny, mud-slick hoof prints have
erased all record of my passages.
The thin trace of trail swings in undulations
past outstretched boughs, skirts an
ancient ant colony and arrives at the
remnants of a logging winch shrouded in
buffalo berry, a sign as plain as my mail box.

A compact cedar cabin, escorted by a
pair of giant cedars, floats atop a
smooth gravel ridge, the gentle swell
of a long abandoned beach.
Three steps up rough coral blocks
left behind by the ancient Silurian Sea,
and I navigate six moss-slick planks home.

My hand pauses on the black wrought iron
handle of a thick, Williamsburg blue door.
A glance flicks left and right, inventories
fish box, net remnants, and floats,
a pitchfork, potato shovel, yoke, and scythe.
They and the rusty bucksaw speak of hard
lives passed here. I am only a pampered witness.

The door creaks open; all is as before, waiting.
Two fogged windows on the back wall,
smudged by the nose of a curious deer,
watch the woods. Stubborn cedar fronds cling
to orbiting red, white and blue braids of my rug.
The antique mirror, flanked by weary candles,
gives me a distorted glance.

Hand tools that shaped this place hang
museum-tidy on pegboard hooks.
A carved walking stick topped by
an alert bird feigning flight
sits in the cobwebbed corner.
Gaudy popcorn tins of seed and feed
await the season's guests, and
wolf spiders feast on the uninvited
at each leaky window.

Protruding nails and softening planks greet
my excursion to the lichen-encrusted deck, but
there's enough life left in them for my seasons.
I pull open the small drawer of the old school
desk serving chickadees and red squirrels.
The large eyes of a nursing deer mouse raise a
frightened question. I close the drawer in reply.

Inside, I slip onto a stiff, ladder-back chair at
the warped maple table littered with
sooty lanterns, spent matches, smooth stones,
and my journal, open to last October's entry.
Pressed to my lips, a pen crowned by
a nail from a deer's hoof, tastes of salty thoughts.
I turn to a blank page, wait for the woods to speak.

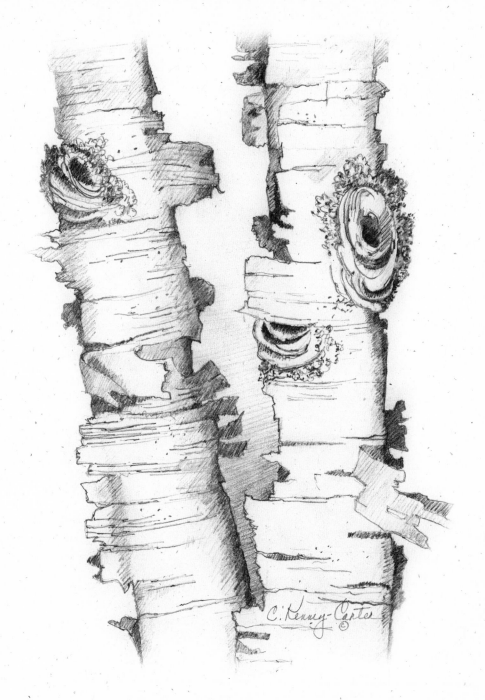

opening a new season

With the first hints of spring, something starts to stir in my body, telling me it is time to spread my wings and join the northward migration. Winter has not quite let go. It retreats for a few days, giving us 60 degrees, buds surging with life, tiny snowdrops beneath the thaw, and optimistic red-winged blackbirds. Then it throws down a fresh coverlet of snow. I wait impatiently a few more days and then must follow the call of the migrating geese. It's too soon. I know, and I have made the same miscalculation for thirty years. But the pull is too strong.

On a bright, promising late April day, I launch in my van loaded with tools, supplies, hand-made furniture and artifacts, and optimism for opening a new season. By the time I have reached Green Bay, all the pleasant, hopeful signs of spring seen further south have slipped away. The green haze of early buds has left the trees, and they return a grim winter gaze, asking me, "What were you thinking?" At least the willows are still glowing with golden energy, as though they were about to explode, telling me I am not entirely wrong.

At Sturgeon Bay, an overcast slips in. It's 42 degrees, and a light rain begins to fall, along with my spirits. The land is still asleep, and I begin to wish I had lingered back where things were more pleasant. When will I learn? Next year, it will be different! Not until after Memorial Day! Emptiness is everywhere, in the landscape and in the villages: Jacksonport, Baileys Harbor, Sister Bay; closed, closed, closed. I could even find a spot to park at the curb in front of Al Johnson's restaurant. Fortunately, a few of the old standbys like Al's, Sister Bay Bowl, and Husby's are open so I can grab a meal out if the cabin fever gets to me. I've got The Pig for grub and Lampert's Yard for building materials, Passtimes for a book or two, and Ace Hardware for whatever. What more do I need? Certainly not the shops and crowds.

Topping Ellison Bay Bluff, I remember the spring I saw slush ice in the bay below, the ultimate disappointment. Not this time. In town, I make a brief stop at Gills Rock Pottery to greet old friends, the Thoresons, and give their border collie, Ruby, a biscuit. We congratulate one another on surviving another winter and promise to get together once I've settled in. At least there will be someone to talk to this trip. Then it's on down Mink River Road to ZZ, and at last to Appleport Lane. As I come around the last curve, holding my breath, I am always relieved to see my small cottage still standing. It hasn't been struck by lightning (again), burned to the ground, vandalized, or crushed by big, cascading birch limbs or wind-thrown cedars. Such foolish fears, but last year, trees had taken out the power line, so there was no heat when I arrived. This year, with the record low lake levels, I worry about the well.

Pulling in between the cedars, I turn off the ignition, open the van door and take in the pure silence, always a singular moment. I try to remember to catch this instant and not rush through it in my eagerness to unload. I take time to breathe and notice, let things register. The aroma of cedar cleanses my city-clogged sense of smell. Other, more subtle scents announce their presence: the damp forest musk of things rotting on their way to soil, and the lake shore's own unmistakable odor of death and rebirth. But mostly I notice the subtle quality of the air that my lungs want to gulp down like pure water from an artesian well.

Cautiously, I open the cottage door, and take a preliminary sniff. Good! No mice got by the defenses this time. Faint animal scents to be sure, probably from my second story tenants, the red squirrels and bats, or an over-wintering raccoon under the cottage. They are ready to move out each spring when I move in.

I light a bayberry candle and smile at the old ritual. But it is about then that I notice the bone-penetrating damp chill of the place. Will any amount of heat ever suck all that cold out of the walls, floors, furniture, and bedding? The electric heat is so slow, and I wish I had a wood-burning stove. All I can do is crank up the thermostats and go find a

little physical work to keep myself warm. Plenty of heavy wood benches had to be hauled out to the deck, fallen birch branches to be gathered up, and roof gutters to be cleaned out. The most symbolic task is taking down the shutters and letting in the first light of a new year. It reminds me to do the same for myself. Time to shake off all the discouragement of winter and allow the hopefulness of a new season to enter. Tomorrow I will clean and polish the glass until it shines like crystal, welcoming the pure light.

Next is the ritual of walking far back into the woods behind the cottage to check out my cabin. But first I have to wade through a swale knee-deep in frigid spring melt-water. That's an initiation into early spring that snaps me into the present moment. "The Word Shop" stands wedged between two giant cedars as though planted with them. More heavy rustic benches have to be hauled out, plus a feeding table for birds and critters who visit my small deck in the rear. The shutters come down, and I labor up a ladder with them to the loft. Steam rises from my wet shirt inside the chilly cabin. One more journey out into the rain, this time to stock the feeding table for old friends I hope made it through the winter.

Everything at my desk is just as I left it seven long months ago. My cabin journal lies open to the last entry, October 27, 1999. A Bic pen with a nail from a deer's hoof mounted on the end holds the page open. Melancholy words float up from the page about a season ending too soon and the many months I must be away. I look out the window and see two of last year's chickadees at the feeder. A pair of red squirrels is also staking early claims. The male has a brilliant flame orange tail and begs to be named. Not yet, in time; we've just met. All that toting of shutters has restored my body heat, but it is the sight of a bright red cardinal framed against a dark cedar, offering his mate a sunflower seed. That really warms me. I pick up the deer pen and scribble my first entry of the year in the cabin journal, something eternally simple about

the wildlife seen this day.

Walking back to the cottage in fading light, I begin to notice other subdued but hopeful signs in the tiny lavender violets accenting the edges of the trail, then bolder clusters of large purple ones, and finally, wildly enthusiastic yellow violets spilling across the apron of natural lawn in front of my deck. They have established themselves in the spaces between the slabs of limestone, thus defining the shape of each step in my walk. Could I ask for a cheerier affirmation of my chosen path?

But by now the rain comes in sheets. The east wind increases the chill giving new meaning to "cooler by the lake." From the shelter of the porch, I notice a large fork of my best cedar has been wrenched off during a winter storm, exposing a strip of its twin's cambium to the assault of insects, disease, and weather. This once unassailable giant now looks vulnerable, the surviving spire still standing straight, yet inadequate and somehow pathetic without its partner. For the longest time, this place and its trees had an eternal quality. Nothing ever seemed to change, not even the cottage. Lately, however, one by one, my large sentinel birch trees, cedars and spruces have been coming down, changing the skyline and its profile. Like me, they are post-mature, and I am reminded that, in nature, it is change that endures, not the particulars.

Time to hunker down for the night and wait out the storm. Maybe tomorrow will be better. I screw in bulbs of extra high wattage brought up to fight off the gloom of nights like these. They help. After a simple skillet meal of sausage slices, mushrooms, peppers and onions, my travel fatigue ebbs away. I have the feeling of security and well-being in my snug little cottage. A new view of this inconstant spring, typical of northeastern Wisconsin, begins to form in my mind. This time is rich in its own ways, the homely pupa before flight, or the tight-fisted bud before birth. I am fortunate to be here as witness, to endure the muck and the chill, to attend the transition and patiently watch for the announcement of new life. The observing mid-wife who really isn't

needed, observer, recorder, that's me.

Still too early to turn in, and I'm not eager to slip between those sheets of ice. I reach for the FM dial, and a Wisconsin Public Radio program, but then withdraw my hand. No, that's not why I came here, to fill my mind with more sound, more talk, as welcome as that might be right now. I dial in silence to still my mind and create an empty canvas for new images, or none at all. Not easy to do. My mind keeps darting back and forth like a caged animal looking for a way out. Some other place would be better: the Olympic Peninsula, the Rocky Mountains, my old home in Evanston, even Oshkosh. Any place but here! I want the phone to ring, to hear a familiar voice.

Leave the phone alone. Let solitude settle in and center you. Isn't this the time out you asked for? My slowing breath chooses peace. Match to the candle, light switches to "off." I let the rain become my mantra.

Dawn is a flaming arrow flying through my curtains, igniting my west wall and the ceiling, snapping my eyes open, bringing me instantly awake. Yes! This is more like it ! My noisy neighbors on the shore make sure I stay awake, as they honk wildly at some unknown intrusion or perceived threat to their goslings. Ah, all is in order. As fast as I can brew a cup of coffee, I am banging through the screen door, mug in hand, to engage the day. Fifty nippy degrees is a big improvement. I stand staring at the great lake's mirror until my hand becomes a claw clutching my cold coffee cup. Such an irresistible message of hope is inscribed on this dawn that it commands response. I summon up Thoreau's admonishment, "That day dawns only to he who is awake." I am most fully awake to this day!

I take the exuberance of the geese for my own and honk up my zeal for a fresh start. Time to haul out the projects I have labored over the winter months: rustic furniture, my best photos nicely framed, curtains my daughter made for me, furnishings in a woodland theme, fresh white shutters to accent the windows and a gingerbread scroll board for the eaves. I have a whole career ahead of me here in reclaiming and restoring this special place, which has been neglected too long.

From the forest edge, an invisible redstart sings his simple, busy little song to accompany me. My music is made with ladders, sawhorses, paint, tools and a happy heart that comes from the construction of dreams. Even with my first simple task, visions of what more might be rush in to join the creative flow of a work in progress. I see the old split rail fence my son made sinking into the soil made new and sturdy once again, picturesque picket fence flower boxes placed at the windowsills and the respectful removal of my vanquished cedar. I see an arbor made from its curving branches and evenings around bright fires from the trimmings.

With the power of change all around me I decide it is time to cooperate, and not resist, or insist on ways, people, places and conditions remaining static because I am more comfortable with the old arrangements. So my big trees are gradually coming down, the lake is lower than I have ever seen it, neighbors are moving away, and new, over-sized homes are crowding in on small sites. Nothing I can do about these unwelcome changes or the inescapable ones in my own life. All around me the accumulated litter of earlier times mocks any notion of permanence. Rusted toys, painted rocks, and empty dog chains rolled into a ball speak of a family grown and scattered. Two lawn ornament geese with broken necks holding hearts in their beaks remind me of a marriage I could never mend. Time for all of it to go. Time for me to jump on the cycle of change and pedal for all I am worth. I can enter into the surge of nature's creative energy I feel all around me by giving myself over to its flow. In the renewal of this cottage is my own renewal.

The sun warms my bare back, as I work on building a screen for the deck and strokes my face when I look up and smile. Now and then, the geese sound off from the lakeshore, announcing their territorial claim, and a red squirrel scolds me from a nearby cedar branch. I remind him where his sunflower seeds come from and tell him I am here to stay. I've got roots here, too, and I am going to sink them deeper.

C. Kenney-Carter ©

in search of appleport

I stood at the foot of Appleport Road where it ends abruptly at the shore of Lake Michigan in a ridge of round, smooth stones a bit too thick for skipping. In my hands was a century-old map of Liberty Grove Township, showing "A P P L E P O R T" strung out in large capital letters from the point where I was standing into the lake. A landmark of some significance must surely been here to deserve such cartographic distinction.

All that I could see now was a "Model T"-sized garage and a few large boulders barely above the surface of the lake. One hundred yards behind me, stood a large, two-story frame house of a 1920s vintage and a boarded-up, one-room cabin peeking out from a poplar grove trying to claim it. I looked far out along the shore from the road's end to see what it saw. To the southeast was Marshall's Point, once the site of an Indian village. They lived lightly on the land and left little mark, except for their bones, potsherds and arrowheads. To the east was Spider Island, a thin shelf of rock that was home to scores of herring gulls and cormorants. The curving shoreline of Newport State Park lay to the northeast. It was once the site of a small, but thriving logging town called Newport. It disappeared long ago with the timber. I had found a tiny, one room, roofless log cabin in woods nearby which bore witness to the fleeting presence of the loggers.

A dozen years ago, I had rescued a nearby, 1930s-style cottage from ruin, chased out the red squirrels and bats, and declared myself a resident of the quiet road called South Appleport Lane. Since then, I had explored the surrounding countryside, the trails and shoreline, curious about that evocative name and seeing signs of another "civilization."

What was this place called "Appleport?" Now I wanted to know who had lived here. What were their lives like? What were the history and links to the living present that I shared? Was it once a brisk little port shipping local apples to Chicago or Milwaukee for pies, cobblers, sauce, or apple bobbing? Appleport, naturally.

Of course, I knew a little about the fishing business that once operated across the road from me. But only a tumble of boulders and timbers known as the "Larson's dock," remained, a low ridge slowly being reclaimed by Lake Michigan. A remodeled cottage next to the dock had been a fish house only two decades ago.

Years ago, I had heard stories around Door County about Appleport, the haunted village. A stranger I had met at a Ridges Sanctuary meeting told me he had slides of all the old buildings once clustered there. "A ghost town," he said. I could find no records, only hints and rumors, nothing specific. Even the "place" itself is hard to find, no distinct boundaries, only a few tantalizing names here and there. Some of the local folks knew where it was, more or less. "Oh yeah, Appleport. It's over east of Sister Bay along the Lake Michigan shore." That was about it. So, it was back to the beginning, back to the land itself to look for clues.

I studied maps and cruised the landscape, drove past orchards and grazing Holsteins on gentle undulations between the shore and Sister Bay to the west looking for signs. I could read the landscape okay, its ridges and swales speaking of the retreat of the last glacier. Where it paused, it left a mound of its debris. Each ridge was crowned with lines of large old maple trees, the kind that, in the fall, make me stop and reach for my camera. Apple trees marched up the slopes in perfect military order. Here, agriculture reigned. No resorts. No shops. No condos, only a scattering of homes here and there.

The most promising signs of "place" showed up about two miles west of the shore at the intersection of County ZZ and Old Stage Road. There, my 1960 edition of the U.S. Geological Survey Map of the area identified "Appleport School." But the daisies stood tall in the unmowed yard, and the swings hung straight on rusty chains. The bell was missing

A. Kenney-Carter

from the tower, and its white clapboard needed fresh paint. It had been a while since the school had heard the sound of children's voices. Next door stood a boarded-up cheese factory, and across ZZ stood an unemployed cherry processing plant. Most intriguing of all was a cluster of perfectly restored log cabins looking very much like a small, historical settlement. Appleport? No. The cabins are authentic enough, but they were hauled out of the woods from remote locations, where they once served as primitive shelter for the loggers who decimated the pine forests long ago. An evocative sign hangs on one reading, "Accuse not nature. She hath done her part. Do thou but thine," Milton.

Returning from my explorations back to my little cottage, I felt I had glimpsed "Appleport." but not quite seen it. I had hoped the landscape would speak to me, but it only murmured its vague memories. What I needed was a live witness to tell me its story. My neighbors were all like me, summer residents without history. I thought the answer might be found about a mile up the road towards Sister Bay at Hazel Larson's home. She was a permanent resident, and her family had been around a long time. We bought raspberries and beans from her garden when we first camped out and started restoring our cottage. The land had been in her family for years, and I purchased it from her son, Wink Larson in 1972. She had seemed friendly and approachable.

When I finally got up the nerve to ask her for an interview, Hazel told me I needed to talk to her sister-in-law, Grace Landstrom. "She was born there, right down on the shore." Hazel said. "1904. She can answer your questions a lot better than me. I've only been here since '33." At last I had found a voice for Appleport.

On my walk up Appleport Road a few days later to meet Grace at Hazel's place, I took my time to carefully look at the details of the scene around me. Leaving my cedar wetland behind, the road led me past wild fields, old pastures filled with spotted knapweed, whose lavender bloom swim with monarch wings in the fall. A few surviving,

but unattended apple trees stood out in the fields as stragglers from another time. In spring, sprigs of Juneberry blossoms break up the backdrop of green on green of cedar, balsam fir and spruce. The steady incline led me to Hazel's land and what was once orchard country. A few gray sticks were all that remained of their once large orchard, and much of the land had been quarried for gravel. A line of gray shacks, the color of old bones hid among the maple trees. Across the road, stood a forgotten tree farm which sheltered deer. The abandoned landscape was gradually trying to work its way back to a former wild state.

Hazel greeted me with boisterous enthusiasm and escorted me into her sunlit kitchen, where she introduced me to Grace. She greeted me with a warm, grandmotherly smile that was at home on her smooth, round face and offered me her small callused hand. Hazel insisted we take time for coffee and fresh apple pie still hot from the oven. I felt like a celebrity and didn't mind taking time for the small talk that followed. When the usual business of family and weather had been covered, she excused herself so Grace and I could get down to business.

Grace sat with hands folded in her lap, her eyes often shining with delight, as she recalled experiences in response to my questions. "My dad came to Appleport about 1900," she told me. "He was a fisherman, like his father before him. Started his own fishing business right down at the end of Appleport Road."

I asked about the big dock that was supposed to have once been there. "It was still there when my dad took over the land. He used it for his fishing business. Went a quarter of a mile out into the lake, all built of timber and stone. Before he came, mules hauled wagonloads of timber and cordwood out to be loaded on shallow draft schooners bound for Milwaukee and Chicago, so the story goes. Sometimes they rafted logs out to bigger ships waiting in deep water. The schooners brought food and supplies to a general store down at the foot of the dock. Of course, that's all gone now. Winter storms washed away the dock."

"And what about the name 'Appleport?' Did they once ship local apples out from that dock?"

"Oh my, no. That's not where the name come from at all. My dad bought the general store from two gentlemen. One was named Mr. Apple and the other Mr. Port."

I felt the story was ending before it began. I had been so sure, but I pressed on with my questions. My wanderings along the forest edge of the forest near the shore led me to lengths of old timbers and pieces of iron being stitched to the ground by twinflower runners. "A sawmill?" I asked. Grace nodded. "Dad had his own mill. Cut lumber to build shanties for the nets and equipment. Packing cases for the fish, too."

"What about the village of Appleport?" I asked her. "People told me there was a town there that had been abandoned, a haunted village. One man even said he had photos of the abandoned buildings."

Grace looked perplexed. "No, there weren't no village. I would have known about that. There was just our place and another family that fished, too."

"But what about all those buildings, the pictures and the kids who said they used to scare themselves coming over to the haunted village?" I asked.

"Why that was just a bunch of our old twine shanties left there after Dad died. They got moved up to Hazel's place later."

I had seen them lining a dirt drive along the edge of an abandoned cherry orchard. They looked like forlorn migrants displaced from their homeland; some still had piles of old fishing nets rotting on the floors. They belonged clustered on the shore, waiting for the return of fishing boats, I thought, not gazing at a dead orchard. Here they were mixed in with weathered remnants of migrant shacks left over from the days of a once prosperous orchard business, forming a semblance of settlement.

Hoping for a deeper history, I asked about the fallen remnants of a small building back in the woods off a rough trail.

"My brothers built a hideout down there when they was just kids. They took a horse and hauled logs out of the woods. Put it all together themselves, they did. Oh, it was real nice. Had a stove and some school desks. One night, my dad went down there to look for them. They'd taken the cream separated from the milk and the ice cream freezer. One was making ice cream, and the other was cooking candy by lantern light."

"We didn't have no electricity, just lamps and gaslights. Later, after the fire burned down the old general store where we lived, Dad built the new house and put in one of those new machines that generated electricity. That's all we had until the current came down there, you know, the high volt."

"What about school?" I asked. Is the one at County ZZ and Old Stage Road the same one you attended?"

"Yes, but I went to the old Appleport school before they tore it down and built the new one at the same place. At that time, there was forty to fifty of us. We was quite a bunch of kids for one teacher, but we learned as much then as they do now. We walked the two miles winter or summer. The only time Dad would come for us was in the winter if there was a storm. Then he would hitch up horses and come with the sleigh. We had friends from the farms all around, and there was a big stone along where North Bay Road comes in. We used to put our own stones on top of it so you could tell who had come by that morning on the way to school. Down where the stream from Three Springs came in, there was a crook in the road and an old bridge. The boys would catch frogs there and cook up the legs. Now the road's been straightened out, the bridge is gone and they put the stream in a culvert. So many changes."

We returned to talking about her father's fishing. "First thing I heard every morning was the big Kahlenberg engine starting up and

C. Kenney-Carter ©

then Dad and the pond boat a chugg'n off into the dark before dawn. The pond boat was different from the ones you see today that are all closed in. It was real wide in the beam and all open. In those days, they didn't use gill nets. They used pond nets, like a big cage. They drove long poles with a pile driver into the bottom of the lake and hung nets around them. You should have seen the fish they brought back each day. The boats was full right up to the gunwales, almost spilling over. Herring mostly, but whitefish, too. The best seasons was spring and fall; summer wasn't much."

"The day's catch was dressed flat along the back, salted, and packed in wooden crates. We cut the wood from the forest at our sawmill and made the crates ourselves. I nailed a lot of them together, starting when I was eight. The Dormer Fish Company would send its big boat down from Marinette and anchor off the shoals. Dad would have to go out in his boat to load the catch because it was too shallow for the big boat to come in."

Grace only went out with her father in his boat a couple of times. In her words she, "never was much for the water." Even though she lived at the edge of Lake Michigan and the family drew its living from it, Grace never learned to swim.

As intrigued as I was, Grace seemed to attach no special significance to her way of life and growing up in Appleport. She simply lived it; that's all. A typical day to her was of little importance. Their days were filled with hard work, she recalled, "But we had good times, I can tell you that."

"In the morning, we had to get ourselves up and get goin', pack our lunches in a tin pail. We had a good time at school with spell'n bees on Fridays, our Christmas program and our big picnic the day school was out, all the games, ice cream, and lemonade; you know how that went. They don't have that anymore."

"At night, we had our work: get the wood, carry in the water and

plenty of barn chores. I was eleven when my mother died, and my older sister didn't stay long, so I had lots to do. When my dad went out on the lake in the morning, he'd call me to milk the cows. Then I'd make breakfast for him when he came back. Once in a while, I'd wait in bed, but when I heard that old motor chugg'n, I got up! We had a strict dad, but he kept us together."

"Later, when I was in my twenties, we had an orchard. I hauled plenty of cherries down to the dock in Sister Bay by Anchor Sam's in our old Model T Ford truck."

"After I was married, they built that plant up there at Old Stage Road and ZZ across from the Appleport School. That's when you should have been here to seen all them trucks lined up for miles, waiting to get in. The cherry business isn't the same anymore. There's no money in it, so people gave up, just quit and let a lot of the orchards die."

The orchards were first planted in the 1920s, and production peaked somewhere in the 1940s. The Larson family finally abandoned their orchard around 1960. All that remains of over a thousand trees are a few dead sticks.

Like his father before him, Grace's dad fished all his life. When he died, his son, Everet, took over and fished until 1966. The catches steadily declined, and it became harder and harder to make the business pay. The death of Grace's father marked the end of one era and the beginning of another. John Larson's lands were divided among his children, and gradually they turned to other ways of earning a living.

The loggers came and went in the late 1800s, and now Appleport is experiencing another wave of change. The hemlock and pine were cut to extinction. The last of the herring was netted, the cherry orchards abandoned, the pastures turned to weeds, and gravel quarried from the land. The fish shanties rot in the woods, paint peels from the clapboard siding of the boarded up cheese factory, Appleport School has been sold for a vacation home, and the cherry processing plant has been converted to winter storage for large pleasure boats. All that remains is the land. Now that final resource is being sold, as descendants of the pioneers take their due before passing from the scene themselves. The land has been divided and sold, and divided again for homes with a view of the lake or a piece of wild roadside. Summer residents, who now settle the land, bring love for Door County and a desire to be part of it, but they bring no sense of history, nor will they leave any. The Scandinavian names will be replaced by a mix of other nationalities. Our children won't attend school together, and we won't be trying to win a living from the land nor the lake. Hopefully, we will remember why we came to this place, respect it, and not hastily recreate the suburban environment we left behind. At the rate land is being subdivided with new large homes coming in, Appleport may yet become a village of sorts.

Standing at the shore in the early morning and watching the few remaining fishing boats pull out of Sand Bay as they have for decades, I am moved at being a witness to tradition and the passing of old ways. An old Kahlenberg engine is still chugging away out there, awakening me in gratitude for another day in Appleport, happy to have found it before it is finally lost.

> To everything
> There is a season
> And a time
> To every purpose
> Under the
> Heavens.

Note: A number of features along the route from Sister Bay have changed since this chapter was first written. Most notably, the collection of log cabins at ZZ and Mink River Road is no longer there, and fewer fish shanties stand on the Larson property.

C. Kenney-Carter ©

chomp, chomp

*A*t the end of our second season in the little Appleport cottage, barely getting comfortable with its rustic, handyman-special condition, nature served up an unexpected drama lesson. Exhausted from a long day of heavy carpentry and repair work, I was startled from a deep sleep by a loud, alien noise. A chomping, crunching sound reverberated through the bare walls, rafters, and flooring, amplified and terrifying in that rather empty, partially finished space we had come to call "civilized camping."

My two dogs, curled comfortably at the foot of the bed, stared wild-eyed at me. They made no sound, nor did they make any move to protect us from whatever was assaulting our fragile den. "Surely," they seemed to say, "you don't expect US to do anything about THAT! We are not going to charge, bark, quietly growl or make any sound that might possibly reveal our presence to whatever monster is out there."

Clearly, I was the appointed one to defend home and family against this unknown terror, I alone. With quaking limbs, and no knowledge of what faceless foe I would encounter, I seized a two by four and a flashlight, sucked up my gut, and stepped cautiously into the night.

The noise was coming from my newly constructed shed attached to the back of the cottage. Something was in there, something unknown and ferocious. What tactics to take in the face of an unknown enemy? Be more aggressive and fearsome than they, attack, put them on the defense, drive them away! "Hi-e-ah!" Slam! Bang! Bang! I delivered splintering blows with the two by four against the shed door. Silence inside. Ha! I had intimidated my foe. Slowly, I slid the door open with the end of my warrior's club and stabbed the darkness of the interior with my sword of light, my breath caught up in my throat. What would it be? Who would make the next move?

There it was, captured in my light. But how could it be? A baby porcupine looked up at me, showed his tiny teeth and hissed, then, almost as a second thought, remembered to put up his wall of quills in defense. I laughed aloud from relief and at my own foolish behavior. How the hell could such a little critter make so much noise? He sounded like he could take the whole cottage down. Guess the acoustics must have been just right.

Now what was I going to do about him? I hadn't moved into the woods to kill critters I wanted to learn about, so I dropped my foolish two by four and watched him. While I didn't know much about porcupines at that time, I quickly learned that I wasn't going to be able to chase him off or shoo him away. Any loud noise or close approach only elevated his quills higher like a massive battery of rockets. And he obviously had far more patience in this waiting game than I did. Picking him up, even with a thick pair of working gloves, didn't seem like an option either. Finally, I settled on an old coal shovel hanging from a peg in the shed. I carefully slid the slim blade under him and shifted him to the back of it. Giggling with nervous relief and triumph, I escorted him a few hundred feet back into the woods, slid him off the blade, and left him with quills at full attention while I hurried back to bed.

He didn't come back, at least not that night. Nor did he return during the whole season, so I thought my coal shovel diplomacy was quite successful. However, when I returned the following spring after a seven months absence, the better part of my new water heater shed door was gone, devoured. It looked as though my porcupine, and perhaps his entire extended family, had been feasting at my expense. I gave passing thought to applying my two by four directly to the skull of my prickly marauder, but that was not my style. Night after night, I waited, not exactly sure of what my strategy would be. But my resolve was never tested. No porcupine returned, except during my trips back home. Each absence brought me less door.

I chose not to be defeated and headed, manfully, for Lampert's Yard and a new piece of plywood. The guy at the yards smiled knowingly, as he explained how porcupines LOVE plywood. It must be just like those delicate vanilla wafer cookies to them. It didn't matter; I'd show 'em! I'd find a way. But my new door got no respect. The same pattern continued in the years ahead. I tried everything I could think of, even creosote. One year, in brilliant desperation, I tried marking my territory, walls and all. I felt self-conscious, but also very animal. No luck. Apparently, my scent wasn't on the registry of ones to be respected. In my ignorance at the time, I didn't realize I was actually enhancing his attraction to my shed, salting it with urine.

As the years passed, I got more philosophical about my ragged door. Besides, it was the only place the porky bothered, and seemed a kind of game. Maybe it was my initiation to the northern forest. Why did the damn shed need a door anyway? He gnawed on a couple of four by fours supporting the roof overhang of my cabin back in the woods, but I decided it added a little flare to the rustic theme and ignored it. Hell, I was the intrusive one here! The critters of these woods were here first, many of them previous tenants of my long abandoned cottage.

Gradually, I developed a curiosity about this odd creature and decided it was time for me to become better acquainted with my persistent neighbor. If we were going to occupy the same habitat and occasionally have our differences, I wanted a better understanding of what was going on. As long as he didn't literally eat me out of house and home, maybe we could work out some kind of compromise.

I started reading up on porcupines and quickly learned how much falsehood there was in the "common knowledge" about porkies that kept getting passed down as factual. *The Stokes Guide to Animal Tracking and Behavior* gave me a good overview, and I began to learn how to read the land for signs of the porcupine's presence other than my chewed up door. Basal trunk scars on my ancient birch trees told me something of their historic presence on my site. I would smile in secret knowledge as I came across a litter of small hemlock branches on my cross-county ski trails. A porcupine with sloppy table manners had been dining above, and might still be there if I looked closely. With limited opportunities for field observation, I picked up bits of information, local folklore and scientific studies. The classic tales concern the porcupine's preferences for toilet seats in outhouses, but wooden handles of tools, boots and tires exposed to salt, are also delicacies. Sodium must spice up an otherwise dreary high-fiber diet.

My local ramblings brought me to an abandoned, roofless log cabin, where the corners were piled high with distinctive, light-colored scat. I could easily identify it as a recent den. Direct sightings were rare because the porcupine is nocturnal, and not very active during the day. I learned to look up for that fuzzy, misshapen ball and could spot one from time to time. It was a good deal easier to locate them in leafless poplars in the fall.

My attempts to become better acquainted through photography, were frustrating and, sometimes, comical. Rarely did I encounter a porky in daylight, and when I did all they wanted to show me were quills, not a profile, and certainly not full face, their most vulnerable quarter. Even close up, not much of a face is visible because the quills and dense guard hairs appear to begin at the brow and ears, and their fur is quite dark. I got some help in this area from another source, David Costello's *The World of the Porcupine*, which has excellent black and white close-up photos. The quill pig's face has a peaceful, sleepy quality, with innocent and benign features belying his well-armored behind. I think they are kind of cute, if rather expressionless, something like a groundhog. I could not imagine the presence of much of a personality, but how would I know? It's not like one might have the opportunity to raise and cuddle and orphan, or so I thought. But Costello showed me otherwise with a charming series of young porcupines raised in captivity relating perfectly well to their sponsors. According to these folks, their young porcupines exhibited plenty of personality and individual differences. They were playful, learned to respond to their names, could easily be hand fed and would even do tricks. One could even lift them by their front paws. Stroking, however, was not recommended.

And that brings us to the subject of quills. I learned about his famous quills, which number in the tens of thousands, first hand. One morning, Kelly, my brainless, "emergency back-up dog," returned looking sheepish and embarrassed with a face full of stiff-looking whiskers which were not her own. She let me pull them out without complaint, only winced, as if she knew it was all her fault anyway. I removed them right away because I knew that the quills with their tiny barbs would continue to work their way in with each muscle contraction." According to Costello, "Many a would-be predator has been done in by these migratory missiles working their way through his body and penetrating a vital organ." Or a mouthful of quills has prevented the hunter from eating, resulting in eventual starvation.

Contrary to widely held beliefs, porcupines do not shoot their quills. However, the quills are only lightly attached to their bodies and transfer quite readily to the body of an enemy upon contact. A quick tail swish in the face of the aggressor or idle curious is a very effective delivery system. Kelly may not have been the brightest crayon in the canine box, but she gave up inappropriate tail sniffing of porcupines.

Contemplating the fierce armament of the porcupine naturally seems to lead to the next question, how do they "do it?" The old punch line, "very carefully" still applies. The exact details have been the subject of wild speculation and much falsehood. In his excellent scientific treatise, *The North American Porcupine*, Uldis Roze acknowledges that few documented observations of have been made of porcupine mating in the wild. However, those in captivity have given us a more accurate

C. Kenney-Carter ©

view of their courtship rituals. First, while their backsides are thick with quills, their undersides are not. The tail and underbody is covered with soft, wool-like hair (hint, hint). Some of the preliminary behavior observed was the male and female standing on their hind legs and rubbing noses. When the female is ready, she backs up to the male and raises her tail. No tail raise, you might as well forget it, pal.

Late one August night, we were awakened by what sounded like a baby crying. Convinced no child had been abandoned in my woods, I concluded that it had to be an amorous male porcupine crooning his love song. If he was successful, then we could expect our local porky population to grow by one the following spring, when there will be something to gnaw on besides bark and my shed door. According to Roze, porcupines are strictly vegetarian and feed on a variety of plants flowers and fruits and vegetables when available; they even graze dandelion blossoms. Now that raises some interesting possibilities.

The porcupine's ability to digest and live on wood fiber enables him to survive severe winters when other animals might starve. Yet, this perfect adaptation has also brought him grave danger. Frequently, he will girdle the tree he is roosting in and thus kill the top above that spot and ruin it for the harvest of long, straight lumber. The enraged reaction of foresters is similar to that of the fishermen to the cormorant and the ranchers to the wolves.

If you combine the forester's reactions with those of the property owners to damage done due to the porky's lust for salt, and you have a deadly combination of enemies. Any interference with man's economic activities or personal property is considered a capital crime for wildlife. Being labeled a "pest" is a death sentence. Many states had bounties on them for decades, according to Roze. They were victims of poison campaigns as well. More recently, "natural" controls have been by reintroducing the porcupine's natural enemy, the fisher. Ironically, the

fisher was near extinction from over-hunting for its fur. We do like to play God.

Of course, man is the greatest natural enemy for all of wildlife, even if not always intended. We are the ones over-populating, over-developing, over-grazing, over-logging, and over-looking the consequences. So, who is really the problem?

I've decided I can live with the various inconveniences that my local critters come up with. Because, after all, I came up to my cottage in the woods to be with them, observe and learn from them, not impose an up-scale life style on a habitat doing just fine without me.

The quill pig is just one of the cast of characters of the north woods, and I have to count myself lucky to have the opportunity to spot one from time to time. A couple of years ago, I surprised one under my cottage when I pulled into the drive. He "sprinted" for the nearby tree line — well, maybe it wasn't a sprint, more like a gulumph. He was about as graceful as a beaver in high gear on land. He had as much up and down motion as forward. When I caught up to him with my camera, he gave me his backside, of course.

For almost a decade, porcupine activity had been absent from my land. I figured whoever had been nibbling on my door maybe got bored and moved on. Or maybe they went back to hemlock branches or poplar bark, like they were supposed to. Then one night, a commotion out back awoke my wife, but not me. The raccoon family frolicking in the loft above our bedroom had kept me awake too many nights, and I had finally learned to tune out all sound. Carolyn thought the coons were moving out at last. She trudged out, flashlight in hand to encourage their exit. A terrible noise was coming from within the shed, so she yanked open the door, and was about to demand what those little coons thought they were doing. Instead, she stood there, open-mouthed, staring at a porcupine the size of a bushel basket, all his quills pointed right at her. Of course, she was sure that all those stories about porcupines shooting their quills were pure folklore, but just to be on the safe side, she said, "Excuse me," quietly shut the door, and left.

Unlike my first reaction 30 years ago, this time I was amused. Somehow, it seemed "right" to me. I wanted to believe this was the same small porky I had shoveled out of shed years ago, that he had come back on steroids to finish the job. However, given that the average age in the wilds is about ten years, more likely, it was his great-grandson. This time, I'm not wringing my hands about how to deal with the "problem." What problem? I amuse myself watching his progress and admiring the rough, bowl-shaped excavation, a signature of the northern forest. I'm glad I still have a porcupine defining my woods.

slaughter of the elders

W hen I first saw what was to become my cottage in the woods, it was the ring of towering cedars surrounding it that most impressed me. They made the building seem like the merest mushroom growing on the forest floor. Looking up at the serrated circle of blue sky defined by the cedar peaks gave me the sense of great depth, as though I were at the bottom of a forested cavity in the earth. Yet there was nothing overpowering or menacing about these tall cedars pressing in on the edge of the small clearing – quite the contrary. These great-grandfather trees seemed to be gathered in a gentle, protective circle, benign elders watching over the site. Their lower limbs hung down alongside of the trunks, and then curved gracefully upwards at their extremities in a supplicating gesture. I could imagine robed holy men, and sense a spiritual presence. There was more here than a mass of cellulose.

White cedar is the dominant tree in this type of northern forest. It out-endures all others in its quest for light and height. The cedar is also known as arbor vitae, "tree of life," probably for its tenacious ability to cling to life under the most demanding physical conditions. I came to admire these tall sentinels and their vast expanse of brothers spreading beyond my borders into a dense forest primeval. Their bark was soft to the touch, almost like fur, their flesh aromatic, and their fronds delicate and intricate. We settled into a long-term relationship: woods, cottage and family, all blended together harmoniously in summers of growing acquaintanceship.

For a quarter of a century, I thought the woods surrounding me were secure. I believed they formed a safe haven for its old cedars to live out their lives, here on this quiet shore of Lake Michigan. What possible threat could there be to the dark, solemn wetland behind my cottage? That mossy, mosquito-infested, impenetrable thicket of balsam fir, white cedar, poplar, and black spruce had stood largely undisturbed for a hundred years. The small fishing settlement that perched on the edge between forest and lake three generations before it had vanished had had little impact. The small scale sawmill that once cut wood for fish crates had barely dented the leading edge of the forest. In the 1940s, a forest fire carved out an opening where poplars and balsam firs now grow. Scorched trees were logged out for poles, but the rest of the forest remained intact.

I owned a three-acre patch on the lakeward border of this forest realm. Lines of ownership on any of my property's borders blended into a continuous flow of green on green. Once in a while, I would stumble onto a rusty strand of barbed wire clinging to a rotted fence post leaning askew, but for the most part, there were no signs of past or present boundaries. This low-lying, wet cedar forest was unfit for agriculture or development because of its thin soils, seasonal flooding, and solid bedrock just below the surface. It had little commercial value. Still, its canopy of cedars, soils, and shallow swales helped the land serve as a great sponge, slowing and holding the run-off from heavy spring rains and melting snow. Fissures in the limestone bedrock helped purify this water, as they carried the flow to ground water aquifers hundreds of feet below.

As far as appearances were concerned, this forest was rather lacking in aesthetic qualities to the eye of the casual observer. Its tumble of branches, thicket-like understory, tipped or fallen trees and wet swales looked like it could use a little drainage and some sprucing up to someone not knowing better.

It is home to all manner of natural plant communities and wildlife: the deer, porcupine, skunk, raccoon, red squirrel, chipmunk, red and gray fox, and even occasional bobcat and coyote. The hermit thrush, red-eyed vireo, redstart, winter wren, black-throated green warbler, ovenbird, great horned owl, pileated woodpecker, ruffed grouse, chickadee , nuthatch, and ruby-throated hummingbird are just

a few of the birds that make this forest their home. As I spent time getting acquainted with the richness right underfoot on a single log, and learned the special melodies of many of the songbirds in the thick brush or right overhead, I gained a different view of the values of such an unkempt-appearing place.

I had wandered the erratic logging trails for so many years that I had come to think of the forest as my own – not as a possession, but as part of my experience with the land of Door County. Its moss- and lichen-covered, chaotic tumble of branches had the quality of ancient, enduring mystery, a hint of the eternal. In this realm of tranquility, nothing much seemed to happen. Changes to the environment had been nearly imperceptible during my tenure on the land.

Then, an alarm bell rang on a summer afternoon in the form of a frantic phone call from a friend staying at my cottage. "Rich, you gotta get up here! You gotta do something! It's just awful! They've got bulldozers and chainsaws, and they are cutting down the cedars! The whole cottage shakes when one of the big ones comes down! Damn, there goes another one! I think they are going to take them all down! You gotta DO something!" He was shouting almost hysterically into the phone.

A great lead ball was forming in my gut. My arms went limp as I put down the phone. Resignation swept me into the nearest chair. I knew there was nothing I could do about what was happening. I didn't own the forest; I only loved it. No matter how I tried, I couldn't visualize what was taking place. Denial perhaps. I was 200 miles away, with other commitments, and would have to wait a few days before driving north to see the damage for myself.

From other calls that began to come in from neighbors, the pieces of "why" started to come together. The land had been handed down from one generation to another in a local family. Until now, the land had been considered of little value, but now the cedars were being cut for

C. Kenney-Carter ©

big timbers to rebuild the family's long-abandoned commercial fishing dock. Through 40 years of neglect, Lake Michigan had reduced the dock to a long pile of rubble. Rumors laced with gossip ran from the dock being rebuilt to honor the passage of a family member, Wink Larson, to a scheme to build condos on the cleared land and offer access to the lake from the rebuilt dock. Local zoning wouldn't support such an action, but with land development pressures and local politics, who knew?

The trip to Door County two weeks after that frantic call was the first time I ever made that journey with any reluctance. It felt like I was going to a funeral. I turned down Appleport Lane with some hesitancy and was relieved to see the same old profile of a curving, cedar-lined road. As I neared my cottage, the damage didn't look too bad. The cedar border was still intact, just a narrow opening a couple of hundred feet north, about where I thought my property line was. A few pieces of equipment were parked there: a logging truck, a yellow Caterpillar tractor with chipped paint, a second tractor on huge rubber tires, and a winch, plus a long flat-bed trailer hitched to a beat-up semi.

I was totally unprepared for what lay beyond that opening. One hundred yards in, it fanned out dramatically in a sudden burst of destruction, like the impact of an exploding bullet on the human body, making a small hole when it enters, then ripping tissue, organs and bone before bursting out in a wide gash the other side. I went reeling, stumbling through this vast, suddenly wall-less space as though I had lost my balance. The hallway of green along the forest trail had vanished. What had once been a forest was now the smoking remnant of a battlefield where a one-sided engagement had been fought and hundreds of the defenseless elders had been slaughtered. There were no wounded, no prisoners, few survivors, only the lifeless trunks and their hacked off limbs stacked high in piles.

I could make no sense of the scene. For me, there was only horror and disbelief. The scent of cedar was so overpowering that it was almost nauseating. The work had been that of uncaring wood butchers. No attempt had been made to thin and shape, spare, to leave something of the forest's character behind. Even unwanted trees were felled if they were in the way. I came upon the loggers, just finishing up for the day, thick-armed, bearded men with sawdust clinging to their sweat-drenched tee-shirts, their chain-saws muttering at idle. They saw my open-mouthed stare of shock, looked sheepish, and turned away. One of them who made eye contact smirked and shrugged. Just doing my job, man. The big Caterpillar crawled away on its clanking treads up the ramp of the flat bed. Then the semi fired up and pulled away, blowing a foul blue cloud that lingered after it left. I stood alone in deep, hush of profound sorrow for a long time.

Eventually, I walked numbly back to my own little patch of cedar trees, to my hideaway cabin to find solace, a place that was still surrounded by the living green of the forest. Even there, I could see through the trees to where the loggers had come right up to my property line, marking it with great piles of stumps, slash and unwanted debris. At dusk, I left my cabin and once again walked through the killing field. A kind of low moaning seemed to hang over the scene.

As the Native Americans might do, I took corn meal to scatter along the way, an offering of apology for what happened here. The white faces of fresh stumps stared up at me in shock. At one particularly large stump of many rings, I took out my clay flute and started to play a few notes of mourning. Even though I felt self-conscious at first, it seemed the right thing to do. My technique may have been flawed, but I hoped my heart was pure enough for the offering to be accepted. A ceremony needed to be performed. No one else was there to do it.

In my grief over the forest, I began to feel a touch of guilt and even hypocrisy. I had built with cedar. My small cabin was cedar-sided, and the decks are built of cedar. At one time, my father had suggested that

I do selected cutting on my own land, but I couldn't quite do it. So, I built with cedar that came from some other forest where I wouldn't have to watch the logging. We need wood, as a resource to live, so maybe there is another issue.

For me, it becomes one of the manner and spirit in which the trees are taken and used. I have always loved working with wood, its scent, texture and willingness to be shaped. Perhaps it is the personalized connection that makes the difference. In our economy, we do things rapidly, impersonally and on a large scale. We take no time to honor our connections with other living things we use for our own purposes. We give no thought to working with love and respect. We could honor the wood that has come to grace our lives instead of treating it like an inexhaustible raw material. When we work in harmony with the spirit of the wood, we come closer to justifying the taking, just as in saying grace over our food we recognize our link to the living world that sustains us.

Today I returned to walk down the old path through my own small forest plot to look again. It has been a year since I could bring myself to go back to the scene. My path is well defined by trees on either side, about 10 feet wide. I have held it open by removing the young balsam firs and buffaloberry that keep trying to reclaim it. This modest trail has been my avenue away from all signs of civilization. As I follow deer tracks in the shallow, wet soil, the path now suddenly disappears, spilling out into the vast cleared opening that was once a dark gathering of cedars.

The overwhelming impression is still one of the visual chaos of a battlefield. The floor of the old path is deep in the bleached bones of cedar branches stripped of their skin by the treads of the Caterpillars. Piles of discarded limbs are everywhere. All about me lay the "rusting" remnants of topped cedars and up-turned gray faces of aging cedar stumps. While not completely a clear-cut, there is no structure left, only

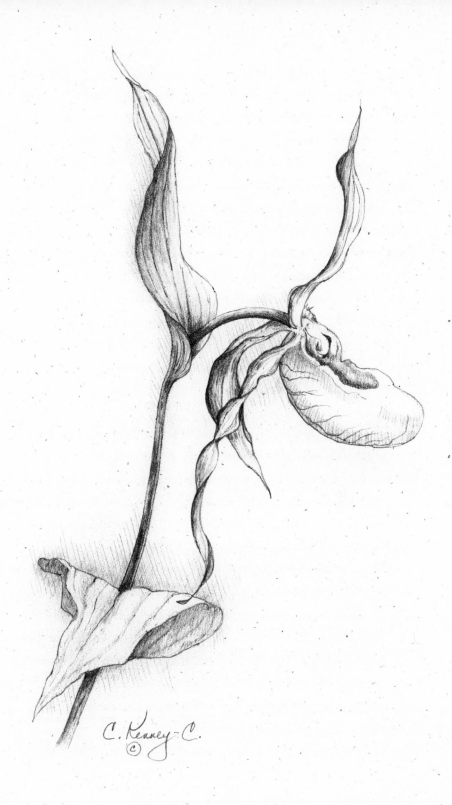

C. Kenney-C.
©

random trees, an occasional poplar, black spruce, or groups of cedars too small to satisfy the lust of the chain saw. Most of the remaining trees are too old and nearly dead, deformed cedars with double trunks, contorted and twisted, bent nearly to the ground. Two skinny, light starved cedars look like grotesque survivors, holding one another up, one with a limb bent at the elbow to support the other.

Now, in this vast sun opening, small balsam fir seedlings have begun a race with sprouts of poplar to reclaim the open land that once was forest. They will take over in thickets within a few years—a swarm of young adolescents massed together, fighting one another for advantage in the light. Gangs of daisies and bright orange and yellow hawkweed are springing up in response to the return of light to the forest floor. They seem excessively cheerful with their enthusiastic smiles, trying to cheer me. They say, "It's not so bad. See, there's still life here."

But the ancient ones are gone and may never return. What is left behind looks ragged and unhealthy. Certainly the slash and clutter from last year's slaughter diminishes whatever visual appeal might remain. That I can walk about more freely in the center of what was once almost an impenetrable forest is little consolation, even with the spread of more wildflowers responding to the light, such as bunchberry, bearberry, twinflower, columbine and swamp buttercup.

I sit upon this old stump and gaze about reflectively. Will this land be allowed to renew itself, and another generation of cedars come to grow to maturity and colonize in the next 100 years, or will it be settled by the scourge of pleasant landscapes, the All-American condo time-share intrusion? Proud new owners will bring in their grass seed, fertilizer, and lawnmowers, reducing the magnificent cedars to scattered landscape design elements. They could aptly name the development "Fox Run," or perhaps, "Run, Fox Run!"

Recent years have brought me to face many life changes and

challenges, and have cut me off from so much I have known: career, home and family. And like this land, I must move through my own succession of changes and resurrection. Unlike the forest, however, I can move on. What are my options now, to search for new habitat and experiences, or remain with what is left of the familiar and adapt?

As I look about, I feel the urge to take over the site, to go in the clearing and remove the brush piles and discards of logging. I want to tidy up the landscape, not just for aesthetic reasons, but so it looks like someone cares about what goes on here, give it a little light management. I would like to collect the slash, the lateral branches, and cedar tops, to burn them in a ceremony of reverence to honor the passing of the great cedars. I would maintain some of the openings for wildflowers, let the daisies reign. The area is more park-like now, and, in time, could be made more pleasing to the eye with a bit of trimming and shaping. Possibly, it could become a setting for watching young surviving cedars gradually grow into adulthood, but not in my lifetime. Yes, I could become the steward for what remains, but I am dreaming, forever the rescuer. I don't even own the land, and there are other plans. Besides, what do I know, maybe the land simply needs to be left alone to slowly revert to whatever new life forms will follow.

Such fantasies come to me as I sit on this stump, knowing I will leave in a few days, uncertain of my return. It has been good to be here this week by myself, both good and difficult. I watch the forest working to heal itself as I work to heal myself. Maybe the best I can do is to enjoy what remains around me now, letting the plants and creatures become more precious to me, learning more about each of them, and learning more about myself as I do. Or, maybe it is time for me to let go of this little island of woods and move on. I feel its shores shrinking and the tide of development rising. Maybe it's time for another cabin in a woods, one more secure, if there is indeed any such place.

In a few days, I will begin an odyssey to Washington's Olympic

Peninsula, land of the battles over the clear-cuts, perhaps to stake a claim to a few acres. Whether I move on to a new homestead in another forest or remain rooted in Door County, I think about stringing up barbed wire and becoming an old curmudgeon, squinting into the sun, patrolling the perimeter, protecting the last tree from the final assault.

in and out of time

*M*y yellow kayak, looking like a giant mobile ad for bananas, had been lashed to the top of the van for nearly a week, waiting on the weather. All the best days of Indian summer had passed, and it felt more like November than October. Door County was closing up for the season. Today was the day I had to leave, to button up the cottage, sweep the roof channels, roll up the hose, take down the screens, put up the shutters, shut off the electric service, and bag the garbage. The sun finally came out and granted its blessing. What a delicious difference! Yet, I had to keep working. So much remained to be done before I could abandon the cottage until spring. Besides, I was waiting for the sweet light of late afternoon. Perhaps I could still dip my paddle once more into the calm surface of Green Bay, waiting to be broken.

On the bluff overlooking the waters of Green Bay sits a rustic cabin peeking out from the surrounding cedars. It is a very special place, a sacred place, that has influenced many lives. I wanted to find it and photograph its face from my kayak. Oh, I knew where the place was and had already spent many hours allowing its magic to work on me. But I had never seen the "Cliff House" from the water. All my time had been spent looking out across the bay from its windows, letting each small pane frame a different picture of cedar, sky, and water. Perched on the very edge of a high rock shelf, that small cabin is not an easy subject to photograph. It keeps its face turned to the bay. Today I would confront that face for the first time and capture one more perspective, even though I knew no photograph could ever reveal its true essence. Nothing in the appearance of the Cliff House speaks to why it is important or how it could have such a profound influence on so many people. Spirit doesn't register on Kodacolor.

All my closing-up chores took more time than I anticipated. They always do, so why was I surprised? My resentment mounted at so much rare sunshine wasted in routine work when the beach and forest trails called. I almost forgot the intrinsic value of the rituals of ending a season. Done at last, later than I hoped for, but maybe not too late. With one eye on the descending sun, and the other upon the stretch of county highway before me, I raced across the peninsula, churning with anxiety. What should have been an adventure was becoming just one more urgent, joyless task.

The shoreline of Ellison Bay curved gracefully out to the forested headland projecting into big Green Bay itself, but I scarcely noticed the beauty. I was too busy hurriedly tugging at the straps that held my kayak to the top of the van. Dragging my craft across the beach, I hesitated. The temperature of the water and the air were both about 50 degrees. Stepping into the water with only my porous aqua socks for protection wasn't appealing, but then neither was the possibility of capsizing in my haste to get my feet out of the cold water. I settled for the lesser discomfort and slowly waded in. Glancing over my shoulder at the rapidly lowering sun, I began to paddle over-zealously. Large, cold splashes of water soaked through the sleeves of my windbreaker as a result of my lack of style. The waters I churned through were clear and tranquil, unlike the state of my mind. Eventually the message came through: "You have plenty of time. Be here. Be a mirror of the bay and not an obtrusive foreign object out of keeping with the spirit of the scene. Feel the grace of your kayak's glide. Move in the wake of the grebes off the bow and in formation with the loons to port." My jaw unclenched, a smile slipped into place, and my breathing became deep and steady. I remembered why I was really here. At last I was back in real time and the real world.

Into the bay, past quiet harbors, empty boat slips, fishing shanties, and shuttered shoreline cottages, I began to notice the rising slope of the Niagara Escarpment. The rocky shore began as a low wall, then rose to a high headland thrusting out into Green Bay. What a handsome,

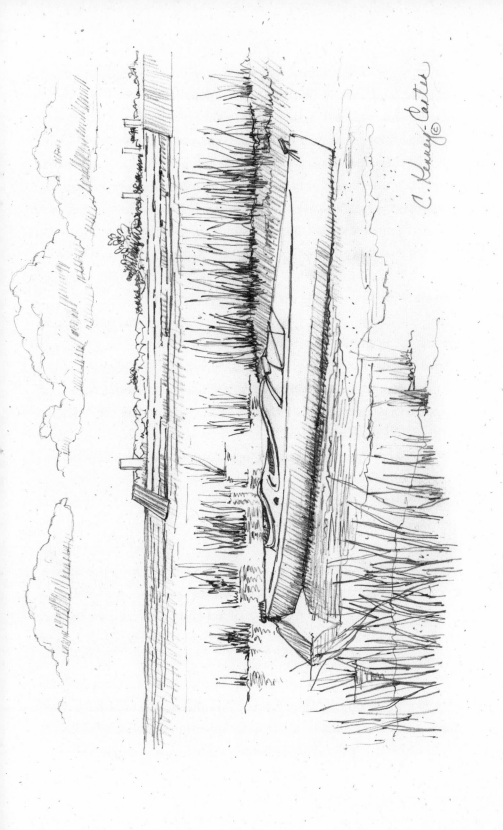

distinguished feature this bluff was in a region lacking the dramatic physical landscape of the West. The sun actually seemed to slow its descent once I relaxed. Time ceased its shrill demands and went silent. I became completely aware of where I was, instead of being so focused on my mission. What good fortune to really be able to se this magnificent setting and to be more than a casual observer from the shore. The scene was a heritage of the glaciers: the clean-shaven jaw of the escarpment, the ice-scoured basins containing the great Green Bay and the lesser Ellison Bay. How hard it was to grasp the reality of the scale of the ice sheet that had done this work! A mere 15,000 years ago I would have been staring up at a block of ice a mile high!

The great warp of rock known as the Niagara stretched out ahead, defining the shoreline. As one might guess from its name, one end thrusts upward at Niagara Falls; from there, it bows beneath the earth's surface, rising once again in Wisconsin at places like Door County and the eastern edge of Lake Winnebago. Composed of a limestone known as dolomite, the Niagara was formed some 440 million years ago at the bottom of an ancient sea and is the result of a vast accumulation and consolidation of tiny marine organisms. The massive rock formation has a distinctive structure that fractures into rectangular slabs and blocks. The mere sight of these rocks can inspire the mason in anyone. Cathedrals, homes, walkways, walls and fireplaces leap into the imagination. As testimony to the inspiration, all along the narrow cobble beach small, impromptu structures appeared, assembled by passers-by. I was grateful that the zeal to build from limestone had not disfigured the Ellison Bay bluff as the extensive quarrying had done at the Sturgeon Bay bluffs.

On the top of the bluff forming the northeastern arm of Ellison Bay is a place called "The Clearing." Its name does not refer to an opening in the woods, but a clearing of the mind. Hidden from sight and melded into a forest mix of hemlock, beech, birch, maple and cedar

is a small gathering of timber and stone buildings. Taken together, they constitute the physical representation of The Clearing, a retreat school that was the inspiration of early twentieth century landscape artist, Jens Jensen. He believed that man's soul withered in city life and needed periodic renewal through reconnection with nature. In the 1930s, he established what he called his "school of the soil," where students of the land could come for a while to study and refresh themselves.

As idyllic as The Clearing's setting was, Jensen had his own retreat from it. I had trouble understanding his need for such an arrangement until I experienced his Cliff House for myself as a modern-day student returning for a week to escape from frantic urban life. This Spartan cabin is straight out of Thoreau's concept of ultimate simplicity. Here life is reduced to scant shelter and basic furnishings. The only distractions are those provided by the setting; the splendid view across the bay and the sound of waves at the foot of the bluff. The Cliff House becomes a meditation in itself and offers an open channel to other realms.

Rounding the curve of shore out into the open waters of Green Bay, I at last became aware of what a solo adventure this was. Not another boat was out there – no sail on the horizon, no iron boat's silhouette, no pond-netters returning with their catch, no Bayliners plowing up a wake, and blessedly no abominable jet skis. I had the bay all to myself in perfect silence. The sound of my paddle breaking the surface of the water almost seemed an intrusion, so I forgot about my haste and let myself drift while studying the high, cedar-topped escarpment. Close in, I could see the ingenious work of cedar roots, clinging to sheer rock faces, and projecting trunks and foliage out into the light above the waters. Contorted, serpentine roots twisted their way into crevasses of limestone, spreading into fine fingers holding on in seeming desperation to support the tree's precarious posture. It seemed symbolic of a heroic act repeated over and over again along the bluff.

A glance over my shoulder showed the sun still hanging above

the horizon, but Jensen's cabin had not yet revealed itself. Certainly I should have spotted it by now. Had I been daydreaming out on these calm waters, so absorbed in reflections that I had missed it? A set of steep stairs leading down to the water just ahead of me told me the end of The Clearing property was near. Just as I was convinced I must turn back, a single window blinked out of the cedars for a moment and then was gone. Seconds later, it reappeared with others. At last, the cabin's rustic, aged face of cedar rounds presented itself on a shelf midway up the bluff. My heart raced with excitement of having suddenly stumbled upon an old friend in unfamiliar haunts.

Mysterious, hidden and withdrawn – how typical of the Cliff House. I gazed up for the first time at the full face of the place where I had spent so many hours looking out and listening from within, pen in hand. Here, so many years ago, I found the courage to claim the poet in me. Now afloat beneath the cabin's placid façade, a profound reverence engulfed me. No grand cathedral, the Cliff House was more like a crude grotto fitted inconspicuously into the scene as though it had grown there. Jensen's cabin reflected his philosophy more eloquently than his own words.

The past experience of my days and nights in this small cabin rose up vividly in my memory. I could smell the wood smoke of its fireplace, hear the sound of waves breaking on the rocks below, and feel its palpable peace. More important, I could recall the profound encounters with myself in nature, ones that put me on a new life path. I had taken many photos of the cabin's simple interior and the views over the waters. Yet, the Cliff House cannot be fully captured in word, sketch or photograph. Only the elusive experience of the place is real, even if hard to define.

I had returned like a pilgrim on a sacred journey and had been granted passage into timeless moments of nature and beauty. How grateful I was I had made it out to location before sunset, indeed, in the perfect late-day light I only dreamed of having. Perfection lay before me. Yet, I was so obsessed with getting the photo that I behaved like a rude tourist. In my haste to start shooting, I fumbled to get my camera out of its case lashed to the deck of my kayak. Juggling lenses and trying to get just the right composition took me out of the peace of the moment and back into frantic time. Alternately paddling in tight circles and jerking the camera to my face for a quick look through the lens was awkward and frustrating. The exercise was like working with a shy, reluctant model. As soon as a promising picture started to come into place, a cedar branch would obscure the full face or the light would change. I began to blaze away with fanaticism in hopes of a lucky shot.

Suddenly, I caught myself again and began to laugh. What an absurd way to go about this mission! In spite of all the peaceful recollections of past times in the Cliff House, I was acting like a lunatic! "Slow down," an inaudible voice from within said. "Breathe! Allow yourself to drift and start really looking at what is in your lens. Let yourself, the kayak, the bay, and the cabin become one, all moving easily together. Be patient. Slow dance with them. The right picture will present itself." And so it did, with a couple of exposures to spare. Waves of gratitude swept over me like gentle surf, as I paddled towards the last rim of sun crowning Ellison Bay Bluff.

C. Kenney-Carter

turkey trot

M y spirits were rising like those of a young boy off on a grand adventure. The tire ruts I followed led me into an ungated field where once I had been treated to the spectacle of hundreds of migrating monarch butterflies descending to clothe the limbs of a large maple tree with their wings as they settled in to rest for the night. Patience and experience had taught me that nature would always present me with some unexpected reward if I were open to receive it. But I never know what will show up or when.

My path paralleled a low, picturesque stone wall littered with dead sumac limbs looking like the cast-off antlers of exotic ungulates. They seemed to foreshadow some ancient mystery about to be revealed. Rusty barbed wire lay prone upon the ground, fence posts stood askew, and their unprotected pasture lands grew wild with weeds announcing the failure of agriculture and the abandonment of the land.

It was as quiet as stones. No one was there to protest my entry. I was free to explore. The ruts vanished into tall grass, not a single blade broken by footsteps this summer. I was at home in an unfenced, congenial habitat with space to roam. My requirements were different from others of my species. I was not a flock bird, a pack animal, nor a member of a herd. I needed space and separation to survive, expansive habitat.

I did not fare well in the crowded coastal villages of Door County. I prospered in the old fields, wetlands and woods of the interior. Here laid the quiet opportunity of secret places to explore – the chance to spot a fox, hear a coyote, watch a deer with her new fawn, or startle a pileated woodpecker into loud, squawking flight and never see a tourist. This land offered a chance to remain still and to see who might show up, and to look at real wildflowers and birds, not just at pictures and posters.

I was grateful to be able to hike into this quiet field and witness nature on the slow rebound. What lesson might she have in store for me? No pristine area, this land had had a lot of hard mileage put on it before being retired. It had been logged and cleared before the turn of the century. Next, it was turned over to pasture and farming. But it made poor farming and, eventually, was abandoned altogether. In ecological terms, it would be called an "old field," land working to heal itself. No more plowing, no more planting, no grazing; the clock of succession had been restarted. The land was going "natural."

Such landscapes had always fascinated me. I had often found them aesthetically pleasing as well, even though they harbor alien plant species that would not naturally be in place if it were not for man's interference. With clusters of trees and open stretches of meadow, the land was reminiscent of a savanna, one of the most universally appealing settings for man and wildlife alike. To me, the groves of ironwood, poplar, black spruce, cedar, and maple were quite inviting. Beneath them, fronds of bracken ferns stood on tall stems, lounging in the shade. Spreading out between the groves were remnant pasture grasses and an assortment of rough weeds. Drifts of Queen Anne's lace, orange and red hawkweed, daisies, and spotted knapweed, once the farmer's bane, had become the favorite subjects of county artists.

No one seemed to be home on this day in June, not even a field sparrow. I had to content myself with looking for coral fossils in the stone wall, discovering coyote scat loaded with rabbit fur, and admiring an unexpected patch of golden coreopsis showing off in an otherwise modest meadow. As beautiful as the scene was, I was disappointed in the lack of wildlife action. I paused to contemplate the stark beauty of a massive, hollow stump of a cedar cut over 100 years ago. It was typical of the giants that once reigned over this land. I was startled out of my musings when a very large bird strode out from behind that stump, not ten feet away. Its long curious neck was followed by a thick body on

stilt-like legs. Nothing flashy in the way of feathers, just a subtle combination of earth tones with wide bronze and black stripes across the body and a pale blue, bald head. It was a wild hen turkey, the first one I had seen around here, and so close.

Her stride from behind the stump was both cautious and purposeful, as though she was coming on stage. The performance she gave was fascinating. And it was a private one, just for me. She cowled her wings as she approached, making her seem much larger. When this maneuver failed to send me fleeing in terror, she carefully extended one wing out and back, dragging it on the ground as though it was injured. Then she paraded back and forth in front of me. I just stood there taking in the show until it finally dawned on me that I was too close to her nest and she was trying to draw me away with the old wounded bird routine. She had her flightless chicks, or "poults" as they are called, hunkered down safely nearby and had come out to take me on. Though it was largely an instinctual act, it seemed a very courageous one as well. If it weren't for her poults, she would never have revealed herself and could have flown to safety if discovered. What an easy shot she would have been, but I had left my large bore Canon zipped up in my camera case back at the cabin. No point in complaining. I just accepted what had been given me, a chance to observe this great bird up close, to focus my mind on its details and behavior directly rather than through a lens.

Her performance was such a good one that I decided to play along. As I took my first cautious steps towards her, her zigzags became more linear and rapid. The accordion pattern became almost a straight line, occasionally doubling-back to make sure I was still interested in pursuit. My casual pace seemed to annoy her. She mentioned it from time to time. What a high stepper she was! Her gait was a strong and determined one, as she led me right out the path by which I had entered. "Come along! Hurry up! I haven't got all afternoon for this nonsense!"

One could easily read human characterizations into her comical, yet serious survival behavior. The well-being of those poults was the most important thing in her life, and she would do anything to save them from this predator. I humbly followed her directions, but with a big grin on my face. Once we neared the exit to the field, she ducked under a couple of strands of barbed wire, did a 180 degree turn on the backside of a line of maple trees and sprinted back toward the nest. I guess she thought I was too dumb to see. Two or three times she stopped down the fence line to make sure I was staying put.

I would like to have accommodated her peace of mind and left immediately, but it was just too fine a moment to abandon so quickly. I lingered to savor the time – seeing my first wild turkey in Door County on an otherwise uneventful little stroll. Maybe such sightings will become commonplace, or maybe I'll only catch an occasional glimpse. I doubt that I will ever see one that close again. It is only a few weeks in spring when the poults are flightless and the hens must take such risks with predators like me. Otherwise, wild turkeys are pretty cagey creatures, grown cautious from centuries of being hunted. They were hunted to extinction in Wisconsin by the 1880s, but have been successfully re-introduced.

Walking out of that field, I felt as satisfied as an old Pilgrim with a turkey in his bag, but I had neither the need nor the desire to shoot one. Just the encounter was thrill enough for me. What a fulfilling afternoon I had had with this small adventure in nature! But I had seen disturbing signs, too. A litter of empty shotgun shell casings did not bode well for my turkey's longevity, but worse, the phosphorous orange surveyor's stakes announced further fragmentation of her habitat and mine. Racks of new mailboxes along my road, awaiting names, had gone up. From the air, I had seen more and more large, ostentatious homes of the super-wealthy appearing in the interior. They gobble up large acreage sites, build over-sized homes to be occupied for just a few weeks

C. Kenney-Carter ©

a season, and close off the their land. "No Trespassing! Criminal Trespass! No Hunting! I've Got Mine. Keep Out." There goes another piece of the whole. The dark shadow of urban sprawl is now on the land where "Nature smiles for miles and miles."

I feel my habitat shrinking, my opportunities to go exploring diminishing. This is what happens to wildlife, and worse, in the face of such sprawl and the fragmentation of their habitat. With their range shrinking and more edge being created, native creatures are exposed to greater predation and competition. Some animals learn to adapt and coexist with us, only to become urban "pests." For now, the turkey, while still a game bird, is relatively secure. It has grown abundant, is fitting into the environment, adapting and becoming a treasured symbol once again. As for myself, like the fox and the turkey, I'll be running the fence lines of civilization for as long as I can.

creating community

WORK WEEK AT THE CLEARING

*A*s certain as migrating geese, we come with the change of seasons in the spring and the fall, drawn by a sense of time and rhythm of life. We are the volunteers for what The Clearing simply calls "Work Week." The natural landscape and rustic, well-placed buildings snuggled into the picturesque setting, seem as though they have always been so, undisturbed. In truth, as perfect as nature is in its own ways and as charming as the picturesque buildings are, both need a lot of care to sustain the image. Only the staff will know we've been here, and the signs of our labor and care will go unnoticed by the first classes as they arrive in awe of the beauty and peace found here. Spring "Work Week" assures the buildings and grounds are in good condition for the opening of a new season, and our lives will have experienced new beginnings as well.

We migrants follow our flyways north, converging on the Door Peninsula with a sense of urgency, drawn by powerful instincts and a desire to return to a place which has meant so much in our lives. While the specifics of our past encounters with The Clearing may differ, the spirit is the same for each of us. Most of us are looking to experience the place in new ways, to give back part of what we have received, and create a pride of ownership through our labors. No one considers the actual work sacrifice or drudgery. We come because we love the work, The Clearing, and the fellowship.

With the first sure signs of spring back home, we can hardly wait to get our journey underway, even though we know it is a bit too early for the full loveliness of Door County to be present. All those wonderful hints of spring around home gradually evaporate by the latitude of Green Bay, except perhaps for the willows glowing with golden energy. Fields of kelly green fade back into sage and tawny tans. Little villages lining the peninsula's highways appear deserted; most business are closed. It's even possible to park on the street in front of Al Johnson's Restaurant. We hope it won't snow, or that maybe we will have a few days of sun and temperatures at least in the 50s, and that the cold drizzle falling won't last all week. Topping the Ellison Bay Bluff for the spectacular view, the heart can go cold at the sight of slush ice still in the bay.

Entering the woods and following the winding drive through Jens Jensen's well-calculated meanders never fails to bring a sigh of peace, allowing our tensions to unwind. Never mind that the landscape seems dead or even brooding; when we step out of the vehicle, catch the scents and the silences of the forest, we know we are home again and ready to be fully here. Thin, pale leaves of an understory of young beech trees still cling to their hosts, not quite ready to give way to the new life. Above them, tower leafless giants of maple, oak, aspen, and birch. But if we brush away the dead leaves from their base, we will find the pale lavender blossoms of a hepatica, and smile.

Walking up the wet path to the lodge, our thoughts are not on the raw weather, but the warmth of old friends waiting inside. Coming through that door always reminds me of the commotion set off when a new flock of geese is greeted by the early arrivals; the gabble rises and falls with each new group. Most of us have been coming here for more than five years, some for more than ten, and we have bonded around these gatherings. Unlike the first evening's dinner for a normal Clearing class, which is filled with the quiet conversation of people just getting to know one another, opening night at Work Week is raucous and loud. The energy, enthusiasm, and joy bounce off the walls. Newcomers may wonder what they have stumbled into, but they are quickly absorbed into the group.

The official greeter is a moocher. E. H. (Ever Hopeful) Wilbur, a black Lab mix, was recently joined by an equally affable golden retriever named Libby. They do their best to make everyone feel at home.

C. Kenney-Carter

The first morning, the energy is still there, and the director waits patiently for a slight break in the volume of chatter to ring the little brass bell and hand out the work assignments. We kid him about not needing assignments; we know what to do and how to do it. Just turn us loose, and step back. For the most part, that's true. Over the years, we have developed "specialties" and preferences, and understand what must be done. Individual volunteers have claimed jobs for themselves. The big, labor-consuming tasks include: washing windows and taking storms up or down; gathering, splitting and stacking firewood; trail maintenance; cleaning up the grounds and flowerbeds; odd handyman jobs, like general cleaning, repairing, and painting. In addition to unfailing willingness, the volunteers bring a helpful range of skills to their jobs. Each season a small group of resourceful folks who can fix just about anything show up. They range from general handymen to carpenters, electricians, and even a retired farmer, who for years had to coax an ancient tractor back to life to haul the wood wagon. They help get The Clearing up and running again.

Although a lot of joking goes on about goofing off, these volunteers have a solid work ethic. Anyone showing up for a free ride is left feeling pretty uncomfortable and doesn't return. Some who can't do as much physically as they once did could feel self-conscious. They have to be persuaded that their presence and contribution matters to the rest of us and that the experience wouldn't be the same without them. Many of us are frankly mystified at the zeal and enthusiasm with which we undertake tasks we would avoid or put off at home. Our parents or spouses wouldn't recognize us.

I have my own theory, one that I believe is shared by fellow volunteers. We are participating in a deeply seated seasonal ritual, one performed on behalf of a place that has captured our hearts and improved the quality of our lives. We are sharing in a labor of love. In today's climate of competition and adversarial engagement, the spirit

of cooperation, teamwork, and communal participation touches something deep within us, something that has gone unnourished for too long. We feel good about ourselves, about one another, and our work. We take pride in the way The Clearing looks when we are done. Though many of our chores are mundane, we gain Zen-like satisfaction with our simple work well done.

What a powerful experience it really is to participate in the opening of a new season, not just for The Clearing, but symbolically for us as well. I know that one of my greatest pleasures has been to remove the three tiers of plastic storms from Jensen's classic, aspiring windows of the main lodge, to wash nearly 100 separate panes and let in the crystal, pure light of spring. Although it involves awkward work on the top of a high extension ladder, I wouldn't give it up without a fight.

The wood crew feels the same way about their special labor. Watching them following the chain saw, gathering rounds and slinging them into the wagon, you expect them to break out in a work chant at any moment. They love the smell of the fresh-cut wood, and can tell you whether it's oak, maple, aspen or birch from the scent, the color of the bark, or the heft. The proper stacking of the splits into piles is an art in itself, one they can step back and admire when they are done. They are strong capable people. If you tried to remove any of them from the wood crew, you could get hurt.

As much as Work Week is about work, it is also very much about food. The Clearing has a reputation for solid, hearty meals, and we volunteers have the appetites of harvesters. We have our own cook, whose great pleasure in life is preparing tasty dishes for large numbers of people. The recipes are outstanding, and we can hardly wait to see what the next offering will be. Homemade salad dressing, pumpkin soup, herb bread and double chocolate cake are among the favored specialties. Food is served family style and passed around long tables. In the true spirit of community, everyone takes a turn at helping prepare the meals, setting up, and washing dishes afterwards. Nobody shirks KP. It's just one more good time to socialize and have fun.

Many volunteers bring their own special treats to share for between-meals foraging. Tins, trays, bags, and baskets of brownies, fudge, cookies, cheeses, munchies, kringles, apples, trail mix, and nuts are bountifully displayed on one of the dining room tables. Each year, certain homemade specialties, such as chocolate chip cookies, are anticipated with as much enthusiasm as the Work Week itself. In spite of all groaning about calories, the containers always go home empty.

After quitting time, our pre-supper appetites are often spiked by a raid on the shops in Sister Bay or Ellison Bay, or a knock on one of our own happy hour cabin doors. Good humor and laughter spill over everywhere and knit us together. With no TV or entertainment center, we are on our own in the evening. The talent pool is surprisingly varied. Skilled photographers often bring their travel or nature slides to share. Writers among us give readings. Now and then, a pianist can be coaxed to step forward and play requests. Always a new, complicated picture puzzle is available to challenge the seriously addicted. Some enjoy forays into art, such as customizing and painting tee shirts or sweatshirts. On nights when it's not too cold, time with a bonfire at a council ring in the company of stars and northern lights offers a show that doesn't play in the big cities.

Oh yes, I almost forgot, the old standby: conversation, the lost art. Topics range from metaphysics to pets or grandchildren. We even have our own comics, storytellers, punsters, and jokers to amuse us at unexpected moments. Our adventures and challenges of the past year find willing ears because we genuinely care about one another.

Even though we may not gather but once or twice a year, it is always as though we have never been apart. The quality of our shared experiences has made us like a large, extended family. Without it ever having been intended, Work Week has become a class on how to build community. Old Jens Jensen would be proud to see how some of his beliefs about working and living together are being put into practice.

At week's end, we return reluctantly to other obligations, back to what we call our lives. Good-byes are hard because we have tasted real community and genuine companionship again. And as we really don't know who will return next season and who will not, it is always, "See you next fall (or next spring), God willing." And He usually is.

skiing newport state park

Gazing across frozen Rowleys Bay from the comfort of a well-worn wooden booth in Grandma's Bakery, I settled into contemplation of the adventure ahead of me. Beyond the bay, stood the tall trees of the quiet woods that form the backbone of Newport State Park. I completed my sacred rituals of sipping one more cup of coffee, reverently peeling off the last layer of an addictive cinnamon roll, and dutifully making my journal entries. Soon I would become part of the scene I was contemplating. But everything was so perfect; I began to consider doing my winter explorations from right there in the booth.

My peaceful "Wah" was unceremoniously swept away by the arrival of scores of teenagers. They assembled, loaded with gear, to board awaiting busses. To my dismay, they were packing skis and might be headed for the same destination. Good, wholesome kids, fun to watch, but our energies were not a match, nor were our objectives. I exited as quickly as I could and hoped for a good head start on Newport's trails.

Pulling into the empty parking lot at the first trail head brought an involuntary smile. On this late February day, Newport was going to be mine, all mine, without a single humanoid to share. I scrambled into my ski bindings, then stumbled over the high ridge of snow left by the plows, as several yellow school buses loaded with exuberant teenagers pulled in behind me.

The silence of the waiting woods under a six-inch thick comforter stood before me as peaceful and meditative, as deep and steady, as breath itself. I leaped onto the ski track, devouring it like a starved beast, exulting in the cleansed air, the perfect glide of my skis, and the total immersion of body and spirit straight into the waiting arms of the woods.

The snow was the texture of sherbet, neither sloppy nor crusty, but creamy and inviting. The only sounds were my breath and swish of my skis, as I focused on holding the track and keeping my rhythm. Everything was perfect, especially the quality of the trail. No abominable snowmobiles here, chewing up the snow, polluting the purity with their stench and noise. In fact, signs even advised hikers to not walk in the ski track. Snowshoers and hikers were given alternate trails, nicely segregating incompatible activities. Made me grin, though, when I saw so many hoof prints right in the track. Deer can't read, of course, but even if they could, they were here first and probably set the trail.

Well into the woods now, and seeing all the deer tracks reminded me I was here for so much more than skiing. So easy to get focused on the performance, style and mastery of the sport and forget my larger purpose. Sure, at the end of this trail I would have burned off the calories of that cinnamon roll, filled my lungs with clean, crisp air, perfected my stride and glide. At times, I really flew down the trail with exhilarating speed and grace. Nice, but I came here for so much more. I had become a machine in motion, unaware of what was around me. Good exercise for certain, good for the body, but what about my soul? Where had my wonder wandered? Or was it in the off position? I deserved more than a workout. I could do that on the dumb machines at the YMCA.

So I stopped in my ski tracks. What was there besides snow and leafless trees and me? These woods were not as devoid of life as I might have first thought. When I allowed it, I felt a great, deep, penetrating calm. The palpable peace of these woods made me content to pause, give up my restlessness and the urge to press on in constant motion.

Taking time to look, really look at something other than the ski track before me, I saw smooth molded forms all around lying beneath the snow as though slumbering. Who slept so deeply here beneath the pure, white coverlets? Ancient rocks, deceased trees, and secret life regrouping for spring. Here and there, deer mice tracks stitched a long

seam across the bed covers, or a scattering of tiny chaff at the base of the stem of a dried-up wildflower marked the remnants of someone's lunch. Telltale stippling light upon the snow showed the comings and goings of tiny critters still active during this time of earth sleep. The arching, worm-like wriggles of the voles' snow caves showed up in shallow spots. In areas of great activity, tiny tracks delicately scarred the cheeks of snow banks in textures that reminded me of the faces of tribal warriors.

A ruffed grouse left perfect in-line prints one behind the other in the shape of airplanes flying in formation. Purposeful, round paw prints of the gray fox stayed closest to the deer mouse trails, while the white-tail deer hooves zigzagged along my own path. Near the edge of Rowleys Bay, where the sun had melted some of the ice, finger-like shapes of paw prints spoke of raccoons, come to drink and wash their food.

I stopped there, too, at wilderness campsite #13. I stepped out of my skis, dug a Power Bar out of my backpack, and planted myself on a rocky out-crop at the shore. From there, I could see the civilization briefly left behind. Had to admit, the fare from Grandma's Bakery had the Power Bar beat, but for now, warmed from the skiing and inspired by discovery, I didn't want to be anywhere else. Lifting my face to the sun, it felt as though it was being held in gentle, caring hands. Hope of spring.

My rocky snow covered ledge provided the perfect classroom for a model demonstration of what would come in the weeks ahead. The sun worked its wonder on the snow cover, softening and melting its edge. Droplets formed, merged, gained in volume, and gathered in rivulets propelled in mass, and drawn by gravity in a downslope run. Charging, twisting, leaping, spilling, more and more streams congealed into larger flows, moving relentlessly towards the level of the lake to inflate its passive mass unnoticed. And so, in time, would all the snow behind me in the woods move away.

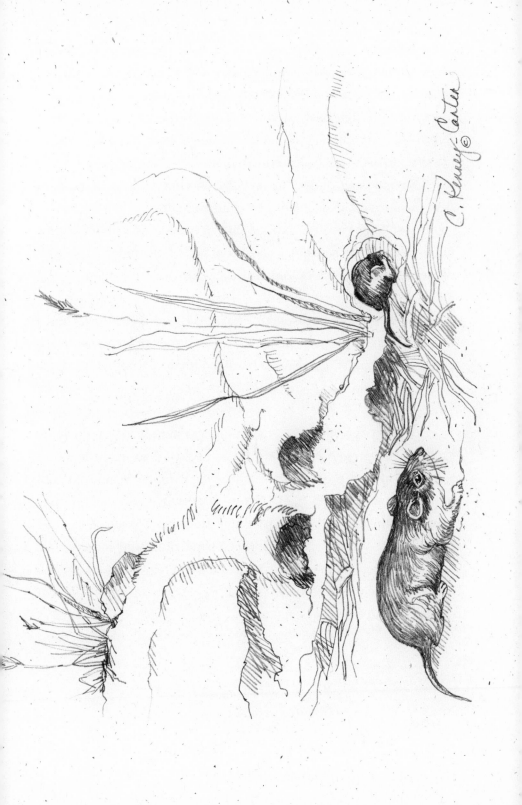

But not just yet. I still had time to ski out of these woods before all that drama took place. On my journey back, my mood shifted, my style changed, became more relaxed, as with alternate sideways glances, I picked out the light trails of critters scampering over nature's sleeping forms. My methodical stroke yielded a slower, more purposeful glide. I listened to the scales on the bottom of my skis "zing" over fallen pine needles on the trail, and smiled at the sound implying a greater speed than I managed. Small botanical lessons were there to be read as well — not just "pine needles," but red pine in bunches of two, white pine in bunches of five, short, flat needles of balsam fir, and even shorter, darker needles of hemlock told me what was overhead without having to look up.

Quick glances at distinctive barks confirmed identities, and I nodded greetings to old friends. An occasional stubborn, pale beech leaf late to fall reminded me that the hardwoods were present, too. Maple bark said, "Hello," and white birch started to peel off a layer, saying, "Notice me!"

Even though the late afternoon sun was starting to turn the snow sloppy, I felt no joy at reaching trail's end after so many hours of solitude. This was probably the last day of good snow I could ski until next year. It would snow again, of course, even in April, enough snow to break your winter-weary heart. But useable, pure, pleasurable snow, no. So I removed my skis with the solemn ritual and mindfulness required of such endings, looked out at the empty parking lot, smiled, and invited the yellow school buses to bring on the color and excitement of new life and a new season.

too early in spring woods

A rude SUV shouldered me off the road on my morning walk today. I could hear his howling a mile or so beyond, and his stench hung like a damp veil in the morning vapors long after he was gone. One vehicle. What about hundreds? Thousands? We never notice when the air is already fouled; we just breathe a little shallower. Still, I was grateful. He reminded me that I do not belong on highways. They are not pathways into the heart of nature. At best, they are blurry peepholes, suited only for casual interest. Time for me to brave the soggy trails where wasting snow still clings in patches, where the frosty breath of the land can be seen, felt and inhaled, where buckets hang from maples, the sap runs, your nose runs, and your heart starts to wake up at the thought of new life on the way. So I thanked the arrogant machine, thanked it for re-directing my feet to where they should be. I was reminded of Thoreau's admonition not to walk on roadways. They only lead us to what we wish to avoid in the first place.

My own sap was still congealed, as I searched too soon for something green sticking its tentative finger from beneath the edge of a brown leaf, feeling for the sun. Yes, too soon, I knew, but my illogical hope said, "Maybe."

Two Canada geese powering around the bend in the river, honking in the boisterous triumph of their return, hugged the tree line, as I waved them by. My kind of traffic. Life was returning, even if the green still slept, except for a mahogany-tinged hepatica leaf patiently waiting for a little more encouragement. High above, the soft persistent rapping spoke of a downy woodpecker's diligent search for grubs and insects wintering over beneath protective bark. Not much to get excited about. I'd seen more evidence of life in the tracks after the last snow a month ago. Be patient, I thought, it's coming, relentless as the next dawn and the one after that. Don't miss this day.

I was cheered by the call of a red-winged blackbird staking out his claim to a stretch of cattail marsh. The squirrels were having acrobatic sex, and the cardinal's song was growing stronger and longer in his optimism. I began to forget about the shades of gray above and the brown beneath my feet. They were merely curtains waiting to go up on the big show. I was lucky to be here early. All the seats were still empty, and I wasn't going to miss anything.

The seductive sounds of a bank-full river drew me to its soothing movement. Riffling by submerged branches of an old willow, it was busy escorting the last flotillas of broken-up ice. I could feel its urgent energy of change. Mesmerized by its movement, I stood smiling, fixed in place until startled by a long, loud, trilling squawk from a sandhill crane standing not 50 yards away in tall reeds. Each loud trumpet blast seemed to come from deep within, ushered with a cloud of frosted breath. No use telling him I didn't have designs on his lady; he was still honked off.

I moved on upstream to give the sandhills their privacy, my skin all prickled with the thrill of the close encounter of the right kind. Two chipmunks sprinted, tails high, across my path and over the moss-carpeted willow trunk. They ignored me, as well as my warning about a pair of red- tailed hawks circling the scene in search of lunch. When you are in love, little else matters. Everywhere pairs, except for me, and a solitary golden-eyed duck floating down stream, all dressed in his handsome tux, but without prospects. We were the only bachelors on the scene.

Keep the rhythm of your hikes, I told myself. Learn to revel in all the fine, early details. Soon abundant life will erupt and leave your senses stupefied. Yeah, there's gonna come a time when I won't be able to choose whether to look up for spring birds or down at my feet for the wildflowers. I'll get dizzy from the overload, asking myself, which warbler is that? Can't remember. An immature, or one I just forgot?

C. Kenney-Carter ©

What's the name of that gorgeous wildflower? I should have reviewed these over the winter. It's as embarrassing as forgetting the name of an old friend. But never mind; there will be no exam. I'll allow myself to be swept away by the total performance. Cheer on the return of old favorites. Savor the quiet joy of getting acquainted with someone new. These thoughts warmed me in spite of the raw air, the sight of ice still clinging to the banks, and the chilled mud on my boots.

I followed the trail of maple pails patiently collecting their liquid treasure. Smoke rose from the sugar shack in the woods ahead. Ah! A warm fire, the welcome of big smiles under furry caps and loud plaids, callused hands offering hot syrup poured over fast-cooling cakes, and the company of fellow believers. What better way to celebrate the Equinox, with all that is here and all that is to come?

going to grandma's

*U*p in Wisconsin's Door County peninsula, in a quiet historical settlement called Rowleys Bay, I make regular pilgrimages to Grandma's. I have been a faithful visitor for thirty years now, and have seen quite a few changes. But some of the best things don't change, and I hope they never will. Still, since time can be so relentless one must not take life's little treasures for granted. My attentiveness is ritualistic, and Grandma's is actually a bakery that carries on the warm tradition of its founder, Alice Peterson. Although she is gone, her recipes live on to please. Funny thing, I sense the place has a special spirit beyond its goodies, so maybe I am visiting Grandma after all.

Bounding up porch steps past the rocker and Adirondack chair, barging through two heavy doors, I plunge through the portal of Grandma's Swedish Bakery. Inside, I inhale aromas of fresh aahs rising from orderly rows of muffins, chocolate doughnuts, caramel-iced long johns, bismarcks oozing jellies, award-winning pecan rolls of heroic proportions, cherry pies, limpa bread loaded with chunks of walnuts and cherries and a host of other dizzying delights covered with powdered or granulated sugar, sliced almonds and other tongue-tempting tastes. But I am a seasoned addict, and only have eyes for one. I know the giant white-crowned cinnamon roll will restore my calm. I slide into the polished wooden booth, mantling my craving as the hawk its prey. The scent of smooth cherry-crème coffee circles up from the slick porcelain cup cradled in the curve of my hopeful hand. Each warm curl of cinnamon roll gets peeled with reverence, stroked with butter and dropped into my waiting mouth, every finger licked clean of icing and lingering flavors. Beneath the ceiling's hand-hewn beams, the clatter of freshly washed cups and sprinkles of light conversation all homogenize with the hum of fans.

At peace again in sanctuary, I allow the landscape painting outside the picture window to come in to me. I absorb the changing hues of blues, greens, and grays of Rowleys Bay, wrinkled, rolling or mirrored. Its moods play out against the impassive cedar backdrop of Newport State Park. Those woods, so rich in their mysteries, have held me captive for hours, breaking out ski trails in the winter or searching for the first hepatica showing off its lavender blooms in spring. But it is the waters of the bay that mesmerize me. With their loud persistent cries, the ever-present herring gulls charm and fascinate the tourists and announce this is a landscape of the lake. Flocks of goldeneyes and mallards salt the chilly surface in early spring. Patient blue herons stalk the reedy shore, and occasionally an osprey will put on a fishing demonstration off the pier. I watch boatloads of hopeful fishermen probe the Mink River's Estuary, recalling my own kayak voyages down its sinuous fingers, surprising grebes and losing myself in the high reeds.

On the near shore, the blue and gold flag of Sweden gossips with the wind and reminds me of the heritage of this place and its settlement. The Grandma's Swedish Bakery that I love is but one element in a complex resort development known as the Wagon Trail. I am no fan of developers, particularly of such pristine places, yet this one was done right.

Leonard Peterson purchased the site as a defunct and primitive resort in 1970. He and his wife, Alice shared a dream to one day have a pleasant campground which would provide a beautiful and wholesome experience for families. Leonard and Alice, along with a family of ten children, took on a true lifetime's work. The Wagon Trail Resort wasn't thrown up overnight; the grounds, cottages, condos and lodge evolved out of a long, often tortuous process, taking years to complete. One of their guiding principles was always to preserve as much of the landscape as possible. The Wagon Trail Resort was planned and carried out by a family with deep roots in Door County, one that respected the environmental setting and history of Rowleys Bay, so the place has a

special feel to it. Hints of its history remain or have been incorporated in materials, though its logging and commercial fishing days are long gone. The wooden cross at the shoreline is a replica of one erected on the opposite shore in the 1670s by a Catholic priest who came to administer to the Indians of the area, a symbol of the county's earliest history. And a school bell announcing the fish boil once called the children of Rowleys Bay to class.

Even without these symbols, I know I am on "holy ground" in the broadest sense. It is seen in the product of a family guided by their humble faith in what they wished to create. It is found in the visible respect for the natural environment. And it is felt in the honoring of unseen connections to the past, the sense of being in a peaceful flow of timelessness. Sitting satisfied in my booth, with the taste of sweetness and cinnamon lingering on my lips, I realize that my well-intended notebook has again remained blank, and my sticky pen never met the page. My gazing has numbed all attempts to be creative on some remote topic. It has left me locked in the eternal present, staring out at the harmony of nature before me. Well, so what? My senses have been rewarded beyond all expectations. Where else could I find such a visual feast and fuel my addictions for three bucks and change?

Note: Since the writing of this essay, the name of the Wagon Trail has been changed to Rowleys Bay Resort.

sailing on the silurian sea

Stepping through the cabin door and walking towards Lake Michigan's shore, I place my feet upon the bottom of an ancient sea, a sea they call the Silurian. Oh, you might not be aware of any former marine presence, unless you were a geologist. My feet leave no mark in shallows of sand, muck or marl. That venerable sea bottom has turned to solid bedrock beneath a thin cover of soil and small stones. Try to put a shovel through that soil and the tip goes "clank" into solid bedrock before it's barely buried. Meet the Silurian.

My cabin is perched atop another, more recent, result of water action – a low ridge of small rounded stones left by a retreating lake, a former storm beach. Lake Michigan is now hundreds of feet to the east. The storm beach my cabin sits upon, and the bedrock beneath that, are doors opening to the complex story of how the structure of this Door County habitat of mine came to be from antiquity to recent history.

All was in place when I chose to build my cabin here thirty years ago. The only real differences are that the trees are taller and I am a good deal older. But my lifetime, your lifetime, and even those of all mankind, are but a few ticks of the clock compared to geologic time. So we don't get to witness the constant, slow change of the landscape. Scientists tell us that this bedrock beneath our feet here is hundreds of feet thick and hundreds of millions of years old, formed of primal muck on the sea floor. This material is chemically precipitated, cemented, and turned to stone, or "lithified," under enormous pressure.

The scientific imaginings, investigations, and deductions of historical geologists always fascinated me. I find myself nodding in agreement and approval as they made their arguments and logical descriptions of what happened millions of years ago during various eons, eras, periods, and epochs of earth building and change. But my understandings are purely intellectual and at a distance. Information often slips away. The question is: how can we experience the feeling of the meaning of living on earth?

Normally, we think of ourselves as living on a rectangular lot in a house or apartment surrounded by a certain amount of lawn and vegetation. We travel on hard surface roads to work and park on more asphalt. We may become dimly aware of a rocky foundation somewhere deep beneath us, if we must pay for a water well to be dug to tap into an aquifer. Usually, however, the whole concept of the earth's structure and history just doesn't register with us. It has no relevance in our busy and oh-so-important little lives, and serves only as a backdrop for our dramas. We have no time, nor the means to digest the wonder of it all.

When I chose a little plot of Door County for my habitat, I wanted to learn as much as I could about it, its history, vegetation, wildlife, ecology, and geology. The question I ask myself now is: can I bridge the gap between my intellectual understanding of geology and a personal experience of that reality? Can I enlist my imagination and yours in grasping a feeling for what we have inherited as a living space, in spite of our brief tenure?

If you are willing, we will cast off in my cabin, now magically converted to a houseboat, and set sail upon the Silurian Sea. Imagine we have turned the clock back 420+ million years ago. Now there's a stretch for you. That's a number hard to relate to unless you are a geologist. Come make the leap anyway. Simply imagine it was, as they say in the fairy tales, "a very long time ago."

What will we see on this voyage? What wonders of an earlier time in earth history will astound us? Our trip will take us across a vast, shallow, quiet, warm tropical sea.

"Tropical?" you say. "I thought we were in Wisconsin?"

Not any more, but never mind; we'll get to that a little later. For now, behold the Silurian. Hollywood has made similar imaginary journeys deep into the geological past. They love the Jurassic period,

C. Kenney-Carter ©

with all its fierce dinosaurs, massive upheavals of the earth and belching volcanoes to terrify us. However, no movie will ever be entitled "Once Upon A Silurian Sea" because there is no drama here. In fact, as far as geologic processes go, the Silurian era is synonymous with sonorous, a great sleepy time in geologic history. Not much was happening except the slow, quiet rain of tiny bodies of marine organisms floating to the sea bottom like particles of dust through sunbeams. They accumulated over millions of years into deposits hundreds of feet thick and eventually formed the bedrock beneath our feet. Through the great pressure of their weight and chemical precipitation, these deposits solidified into rocks. Limestone and dolostone (a tougher cousin to limestone) make up the bedrock and distinctive outcrops we see today along the east shore of Green Bay.

Assuming we could have lived a few million years to observe this process, it would make watching the grass grow seem like an aerobic workout. Still, be patient; sail on with me to see what we might discover. After all, the Silurian Sea was a tropical sea and this was known as the "age of coral," bringing up images of islands, reefs, and tropical paradise.

Here in Door County, the evidence is all around us, if we know what to look for. The fossilized remains of coral life are everywhere, on rocky beaches, in the bedrock, and in the stone fences that border fields. I have been collecting them for years, fascinated by the forms and intricate patterns found in chain coral, organ pipe coral, honeycomb coral, and horn coral. Pick up a rock from a farmer's field, and feel its texture. It will remind you why one doesn't walk barefoot on coral.

Should our cabin houseboat run aground on a coral reef, atoll or island, we wouldn't be greeted by hip-swaying, permissive Polynesians like the crew of the H. M. S. Bounty. We are much too early in time for such complex creatures. The Great Creator is still busy amusing himself with his tropical fish tank and has many more millions of years to get bored enough to come up with more dangerous life forms. Even these coral communities, while they have many fascinating creatures, are not nearly as diverse as found in today's coral seas. Still, leaning over the deck and peering into the shallows, we would glimpse fascinating creatures — sea lilies, cephalopods, trilobites, snails, clams, sea scorpions, and brachiopods, in addition to many forms of coral. One of the top predators of the time, a long, tapered cephalopod, is an exotic-looking creature resembling an octopus wearing a dunce cap.

Returning to our coral reef in Appleport, Door County to reflect on what we have seen, we are left with an intriguing question. What are coral fossils doing up here in Wisconsin? After all, there is nothing conducive to tropical growth in northern Wisconsin. Early on, the presence of these corals was a puzzle to scientists, who could only mumble something about inexplicable climatic changes being the possible cause.

Since the late 1960s, however, broad acceptance of the continental drift theory and plate tectonics has offered a more plausible explanation – plausible, but difficult to imagine in human terms. The continents, once joined together, have been drifting apart and now occupy different locations. Our piece of the Silurian Sea bottom, that eventually became land, was once located near the equator. The rocks and corals forming this landmass migrated up to their present location over several millions of years. In other words, here wasn't here when it was formed.

Perhaps one way to envision this process is to think of the earth as a giant toasted marshmallow, maybe about the size of a beach ball for scale. When cooled, the thin fragile crust (our sturdy bedrock) floats upon a mobile plastic mantle. This bedrock, this solid, unyielding, reliable, foundation on which we live out our lives came slip-sliding up to the steadfast Midwest from a long way away. That's a bit unsettling. Are we still moving and don't know it?

To check out the idea, I went down to the lake shore where a big slab bedrock has been exposed by low water, and jumped on it a couple of times. You know, like trying to slide a rug in place. It didn't budge. I feel better now. Of course, if these plates are moving at the rate of only a few inches a year, it's not like that would register with our meager senses.

If we can conceive of the continents breaking and drifting apart, moving great distances and coalescing again, then it should be no stretch to visualize a few layers of sedimentary rocks being folded and tilted by great pressures from deep beneath the earth's surface. The structure we see today along the Door Peninsula is the result of a whole range of geologic forces that have made dramatic changes to create the present landscape. These forces include uplift, erosion, and glaciation. The headlands we admire so much, like Ellison Bay Bluff and Eagle Bluff, are parts of a distinct layer of dolostone called the Niagara that was created during our now familiar Silurian period. Individual bands of rock are called formations and identified by names derived from prominent locations or places where they have been studied, Niagara Falls in this case.

The Niagara formation is warped in an extensive, bowl-like structure known as the Michigan Basin. In Wisconsin, its upward-tilted edge forms a steep cliff called an escarpment. Standing atop one section of this escarpment, we can see straight down to the waters of Green Bay, but one's senses cannot pick up the gentle slope of the Niagara formation to the east. At the Lake Michigan shore, the formation appears to lie flat as a midwestern highway, but it dips gently to the east, goes under Lake Michigan, and emerges at Niagara Falls in New York. The Niagara dolostone is but one of several layers composing the structure of this vast basin. It is dominant and most visible to us because it is composed of rocks more resistant to erosion. Other, softer exposures of surrounding sedimentary formations have been worn away.

In visualizing this structure, you might think of a broad, shallow bowl formed through the lamination of different harnesses of wood of varying thickness all warped and cemented together and tapered to a tough oak edge. Imagine burying the bowl and filling it so only the oak edge was showing. We might have a crude model of the structure beneath our feet on the Door Peninsula.

As dramatic and inspiring as these series of bluffs along Green Bay are, the upthrust of these bold faces is but one more chapter in the shaping of this landscape we love so much. All of the ancient history of the land still awaited another touch of the Great Craftsman's hand, a flourish of glaciation.

The Ice Age (or Pleistocene Epoch) began some 1.8 million years ago and concluded only 11,500 years ago, when the ice retreated from Door County. For me, visualizing vast sheets of ice a mile high advancing and retreating is a good deal easier than relating to continental drift sliding my home base around. After all, if you live in northern Wisconsin, you have experienced certain winters when you are convinced that this is the year that marks the beginning of the next ice age. Besides, when the last glacier retreated from Wisconsin, it was just a few thousand years ago, and man was on the scene. Some of the guys from around Green Bay were hunting mastodons with crude spears long before pursuing white tails with high tech weapons.

The glacier has often been described as nature's bulldozer. With its massive weight and abrasive power, it can carve up mountain ranges; gouge out basins for lakes and level terrain, as it moves irresistibly forward. Glaciers are the great rearrangers of stage settings wherever they go. Upon retreat from climatic warming, they return all that they have taken from the land, but not to the same places, or in the same forms. They take from one area and give to another. In the more northern areas near their origins, they mostly scraped and scoured the land. Even in Door County, they were stingy with their deposits, leaving

only thin deposits of soil on top of bedrock compared to the deeper soils inherited in more southern Wisconsin. As a glacier melts, it spreads debris, creating thick, rich deposits, dumps other debris to form distinctive hills called moraines, eskers, or kames, and creates a subdued terrain. Rivers are diverted, lakes and wetlands created. An interrupted pattern of drainage is one of the glacier's distinctive calling cards. Forests exiled by the ice begin to reoccupy the land along with other displaced vegetation and wildlife. This is Wisconsin as we know it.

If it were not for the glaciers, the Niagara Escarpment would likely form a more continuous rock rim. Giant lobes of ice moving out of Canada scooped out the Green Bay and Lake Michigan basins. They followed the path of least resistance, grinding up softer sedimentary rocks and excavating former river valleys. Once again, the sturdy dolostone stood firm against the ice scour, taking the punishment, but encouraging the ice to slide on by, directing it to former river bodies where the going was easier. As a result, we now have paired bays on each side of the peninsula, aligned northwest : Eagle Harbor/ Baileys Harbor, Sister Bay/North Bay, and Ellison Bay/Rowleys Bay. From the tower high above Eagle Bluff in Peninsula State Park one can see a whole series of headlands and harbors where tongues of ice cut through the peninsula from the Green Bay lobe.

The story of complex events creating the present day landscape is a stretch for the human mind's capacity to comprehend. Our personal references of scale and time are so limited that it is difficult for us to relate to except in detached, theoretical or scientific terms, and few of us have that capacity.

Still, when I walk my Appleport trails leading from my cabin door, kick a chunk of chain coral with my boot, I pick it up and smile in recognition. I can have a fleeting appreciation for a piece of my local earth turf formed in tropical seas far away unfathomable years ago, and at least muse, "How about that?" When I admire the rugged bluff faces watching over Green Bay, I can enjoy a sketchy diagram in my mind's eye of how they came to be in the big warp and subsequent erosion. Entering Ellison Bay in my kayak, I can visualize the glaciers scooping out the deep basins, then filling them up with chilly waters as they melted from the scene. Flying over the peninsula in my Cessna, I see beyond the villages, orchards, fields and roads to gain a deeply satisfying perspective on how its distinctive form came to be. If only for a moment, I get a feeling of being part of a long journey of change rather than a brief flash of light in a stationary setting. I doff my cap and say, "Thank you," with heart-felt gratitude.

the joys of restoration

SAVING THE SAWYER CREEK SAVANNA

When I first came from the Chicago area to Oshkosh a few years ago, it was to help restore old airplanes at the Experimental Aircraft Association, a real passion of mine. Stumbling on an opportunity to re-engage a second passion was completely unexpected. I had only been there a few days when I decided to take a little stroll near my apartment on Westfield Street. I walked past the World War II tanks forming monuments at Red Arrow Park with its sprawling Little League baseball diamonds. Approaching a bridge that crossed a small creek, I was surprised to find two boys dangling fishing lines into the water. What could the little optimists possibly expect to catch in a shallow urban stream loaded with algae? But the limbs of an ancient oak extended shade over the water, creating a pleasant play of light and shadow on the surface. Well, I thought, at least they had an attractive spot in which to fantasize.

Once across the bridge, I came upon a gravel path wandering along the creek, leading into open woods. This was my kind of habitat, and right here in the city! The further I went, the more excited I got. Clutches of wild geranium and starry Solomon's seal accented the edges of the path. Here and there, I saw tall stands of woodland sunflowers and goldenrod scattered in openings between widely spaced hickories and oaks. Birds flitted everywhere. This was no mere scruffy patch of woods. Here nature was fully alive. This was, in fact, a rare prairie remnant, an oak savanna! Even so, ominous signs of the relentless march of aggressive buckthorn and honeysuckle were distressing. They were well on their way to overwhelming the natives.

Who owned this place, I wondered? Did they know what they had here? Was it safe from development? Were they aware of how the alien shrubs were rapidly overgrowing the place? Could I convince them to do something about it before it was too late?

Before coming to Oshkosh, I had volunteered for several years in the Chicago area Forest Preserves as part of a movement to recover and restore their precious savannas. Only recently coming into full recognition, these extensive woods are called "The Chicago Wilderness." They are one of the largest concentrations of oak savanna in the country, an extremely rare ecosystem. Here I was in Oshkosh, finding one right outside my door! Guess there was no escaping it, opportunities for restoration work of all kinds were both in my face and in my blood.

Gradually, I met others on my walks that shared my interests and concerns. These included: residents of the Evergreen Retirement Community, the entity who owned the land; the president of the Wild Ones natural landscaping organization; neighbors of the site; and even the head of the grounds crew for Evergreen. It seemed as though the idea of saving and restoring this site was occurring simultaneously to almost everyone who knew anything about it.

We organized and met with Evergreen representatives to plan strategies and execute a work program in a spirit of great enthusiasm and open cooperation. Even the DNR contributed scientific expertise, once we were organized. We called ourselves the Friends of the Sawyer Creek Savanna, took up arms and began the long campaign to take the savanna back from its enemies. We wanted to encourage native plants still hiding in old seed banks to emerge again and flourish. It seemed that something deep within us was responding to an ancient call.

So what is a savanna anyway, and why should anyone care if one is restored? Usually we think of the grasslands of Africa when we hear the term "savanna," but the term applies equally well here. Before European settlement, vast areas of Wisconsin were covered with woods, prairies, and combinations of the two, known as savannas. Often they were also called "oak openings." Savannas are not mere patches of woods; they are distinct plant communities with a great diversity of

species. They were the transition zones between the drier open prairies of the West and the closed-canopy forests that once existed throughout the Midwest. Today, in a nation that still waxes romantic about its prairies, only one tenth of one percent of them remain. The same figure applies to the oak savannas, making them one of the rarest of the rare ecosystems. Our Sawyer Creek Savanna may only cover six and a half acres, but it is a precious piece of land.

My daily walks through this little Oshkosh savanna began to demonstrate what we mean when we say such areas are diverse. Add in a little stream, and the wealth of the life really multiplies. Not only did I discover scores of different wildflowers, grasses and sedges but muskrats would swim right up to the bank where I was standing, and beavers would give the water a tail slap, then dive when I passed by. Turtles sunned themselves on fallen willow branches, while overhead, kingfishers dove out of willow trees to catch breakfast on the fly. Most mornings, my walk would launch a great blue heron from his quiet fishing spot. I even saw an osprey circle from time to time. Chipmunks darted across my path. Moles, voles, deer mice, and rabbits called this place home, as did songbirds, woodpeckers, owls and hawks. Waves of wildflower blossoms came alive with bees, butterflies and other nectar-seeking insects. That is what made a place like this so appealing to me: the experience of constant discovery and the vibrating aliveness of it, all awash in color.

Contrast a scene like this with typical public parks or landscaped institutional lands. All you find there are a few remnant oaks and acres of closely mowed grass. The only wildlife present are colonies of squirrels, the ubiquitous crows, and a few robins on the lawn pulling up tainted worms.

One can see remnants of the oak savannas in overgrazed wood lots of farms and in any city with " park, oak, or grove" in its name. But their plant diversity has been erased. Only the trees remain, and they are not replacing themselves. The natural beauty of the savanna has always held great appeal for man as his own habitat, but that popularity has brought on near extinction through development and over-farming. We have squandered more than a national heritage and resource. We have lost, in a way, a part of ourselves in the process, and most of us are not even aware of it.

As a kid growing up in the Chicago area, I roamed those forest preserves without much thought about them. I was no budding botanist. All I knew was that simply being there felt good. That feeling was a clue that something deeper was going on inside of me, a kind of ancient connection of which I had no knowledge. I responded to the wildness of it all, the surprises and discoveries of a world so different from the tameness of suburbia and its predictable sameness.

My mom had grown up on the prairies around the turn of the century and used to talk about the beauty of the wildflowers and grasses. I wondered if they could be the same ones I was seeing. So in my college years, I started taking her out on Mothers' Day to see what was happening in the woods. Her joy and enthusiasm began to deepen my own appreciation for these secret places. I lost my opportunity to do much further exploration as I grew older, but my major in geography and subsequent post-graduate work kept my appreciation for the earth alive. Even when I took my academic work into the field of city planning, establishing parks and open spaces became a specialty for me. But I lost my lust for wildness in the thrust of urban practicality. It took a full circle of my career path to bring me back to the magic.

As I began to search for escape from the too-muchness of the city, even resorts at scenic places could not satisfy the restlessness for something more than mere vacation. It was not until I bought a run-down cottage on the edge of a wetland that I knew the wildness was calling me home. And it was not until early retirement and a return to graduate environmental studies that I was introduced to the soul-satisfying work of restoration. Pioneering work in the rediscovery, appreciation, and restoration of prairies and savannas of the Chicago area was going on at that time, and some of the professors at Northeastern Illinois University, where I studied, were leaders in the movement. They got us out of the classroom and into the field, encouraged us to do hands-on work as volunteers with The Nature Conservancy and North Branch Prairie Project. I never would have guessed that I would have so much enthusiasm for such a late-life venture.

It is ironic that the value of prairies and savannas is starting to be appreciated only as they near extinction. Now we face not only the challenging mission of trying to preserve what we still have, but the equally daunting task of bringing those few ragged remnants back to good health. Because the complex nature of prairie ecology has been so greatly disturbed, it will take an intensive, human-directed effort to assist them in their comeback.

Savannas are not static plant communities; they are highly dynamic. For them to prosper, there must be a balance of light and shade. The oaks and hickories must be spaced widely enough to allow light for the grasses and flowers to flourish, but that same light also encourages woody plants to grow. Unchecked, they will eventually shade out the flowers and grasses.

Originally, grazing buffalo and occasional grass fires kept the "woodies" down, but with the coming of the white man, the buffalo were nearly exterminated, and the fires were suppressed. The open areas then faced an even greater challenge with the introduction of exotic plants, which could out-compete native species in the contest for light.

Buckthorn, in particular, has become the scourge of the American woods and savannas. This plant was imported from Europe as a natural fence and screening shrub. Its thick, rapid growth and tolerance of shade makes it a fierce competitor. Buckthorn is the first to leaf out in

the spring and the last to lose its leaves in the fall. Once established, nothing can grow beneath its shade, and as the older trees die, all that is left is a buckthorn desert. Other problem aliens, such as Eurasian honeysuckle, garlic mustard and purple loosestrife, are also creating serious challenges for our natural areas. The campaigns to eliminate the threats from alien species often amount to a kind of warfare.

I can't help but notice just how combative the language of restoration is. It could serve as script for a science fiction adventure. We are engaged in a war with "invasive alien species," creatures which are hard to kill, who keep coming back. We are still on the learning curve when it comes to discovering how to eliminate them altogether. In the meantime, we employ all means, fair or foul. It often feels like hand-to-hand combat. Early in our Sawyer Creek campaign, one of our buckthorn warriors waded into a big stand of the stuff with his chainsaw. He emerged out the back side with a big grin on his face, but was bleeding from three places.

We use the blade and the torch; we wrench them out by the roots, and even resort to chemical warfare. When all that moves too slowly, we call in a "tank," the big brush hog. It's sort of like a power mower on steroids. You flip the switch, engage the gears and hang on as it charges over the buckthorn chopping it up and hurling fragments aside.

Restoration work can be physically hard and labor intensive. But I have found sheer joy in taking physical action to set a prairie or savanna free from the occupying force of destructive aliens. You have no idea how good it can make you feel until you have tried it and seen the results. It is all a battle for the light. To be an agent for returning the light to the savanna and witness the grateful explosion of colorful native plants makes one feel like a conquering hero. We experience the satisfaction of setting something right that had been wrong too long.

That was our reaction after brush hogging the Sawyer Creek Savanna. We leveled the playing field as far as availability of light was

R. Kenney-Carter ©

concerned. The response of native wildflowers whose seed banks had been waiting patiently in the soil for years was stunning. All of the savanna was transformed. Species after new species appeared throughout the growing season in a constant change of color, plumes of white, petals of purple, splashes of gold, and drifts of lavender flowed through the site, far exceeding our expectations.

Unfortunately, the war is not over. The behavior of buckthorn reminds me of a scene in an Arnold Schwarzenegger movie, "The Terminator," where Arnold tells the desk sergeant, "I'll be back." If the cuts aren't treated with herbicide, buckthorn re-sprouts like a hydra-headed monster. So, each year for several years, we will have to cut, treat, pull, burn, and mow until the native plants are fully re-established again. Eventually, the buckthorn, honeysuckle, burdock, thistle, sweet clover, crown vetch and other aliens will no longer dominate.

Of course, not all restoration work is combative. I have found caring for a site with patient stewardship over long periods to be nurturing for both the land and its caregiver. The sensuous, soft silkiness of Indian grass seeds passing through my hands back into the land always makes me smile. Carefully stamping the loose earth around a seedling or transplant carries with it encouragement, as well as an expression of hope and faith in the future. Any good gardener knows these joys, as well as the bond between himself and the land. Yet there is something more that comes from restoration – that special satisfaction that comes from seeing even small pieces of the natural landscape brought back to life.

mourning the dove

Mid-May, and I am just settling into my little trailer on the vast campground of the Experimental Aircraft Association in Oshkosh, Wisconsin, months ahead of the annual gathering of airmen, builders, restorers, and aviation enthusiasts. By late July, I will be camped out with fifty thousand fellow aviators and their families here for the week's convention of workshops, lectures, displays, and, of course, flying. Upwards of three quarters of a million people will pass through the gates, and some thirteen to fifteen thousand airplanes will land during that time. But for now, it is quiet. Only a handful of trailers are parked in the area reserved for the volunteers, like myself, who come early and work for weeks to set up the grounds and facilities for the massive migration to follow.

On my first morning's walk to the showers, I spot the nest of a mourning dove perched atop the air conditioner for the bunkhouse, where some of the volunteers camp out. I wonder if she has any idea of how much traffic is going to be passing within just a few feet of her nest. Of course, her brood will have fledged long before any serious crowds show up. She regards my close passage with a fearful look, but stays put. I smile thinking of what pleasure I will have in the days ahead watching her chicks hatch, feed and grow. Maybe I will even get to see them launch into flight.

Each day I look forward to my trips past the nest, admiring her tawny loveliness, accented by the black comma on her cheek. She becomes more accustomed to my presence and no longer weighs the possibility of fleeing the nest at my approach. How appropriate for her to be here with us, as we gather to celebrate man's 100th year of flight. Her ancient ancestors began it all, and she is the perfect symbol. I recall seeing in a museum, a graceful, bird-shaped airplane they named the Taube Dove that dated back to 1914. And I remember the call of the mourning doves of my youth, waking me on summer mornings, with their call and the whistle of their wings in flight. How rewarding it is to be re-united here. I have so much to look forward to.

Sadly, it isn't going to turn out as I imagined. Now the nest is empty, remains empty, will never come alive again. I see her lovely body lying limp and lifeless a few feet away. How?! Sorrow and rage spiral upward together, as the accuser in me searches for a perpetrator. Some damn, overzealous maintenance man took exception to her untidy presence. Or maybe it was one of those hunters who lust after killing this beautiful bird. No, I am wrong, too quick to judge. Slowly looking up, I see the darkened window of the bunkhouse in the early morning light. Behind it, the dim red night-light barely illuminates the interior. In the dust on the glass, her faint image, wings held in a high V, is just visible. This was the first night the light had been turned on, making the window appear like an opening she could fly through on her way to the nest.

I will still think of her each time I pass the bunkhouse this summer, and of the brood that will never come to their own full-feathered flight. Such are the risks in nature, in flight, and in life. Another dead bird, breaking its neck trying to fly through a window. Happens all the time. So what? Still this one touches me with unexpected grief. Why? If her image keeps returning, there's a reason, and I need to pay attention.

She is a messenger, reminding me to incubate my own unborn potential and to treasure my privilege to fly. This winter I will go to Tucson and fulfill a long-held desire to master the art of quiet flight in a glider. She inspires me to follow her form and learn how to soar. Perhaps my wings will also whistle. I choose to think of her with less sadness now. She died doing what she was meant to do, and should I happen to depart the same way, well that will be okay.

C. Kenney-Carter

end of a season

A black spruce, one of the tall sentinel trees that stood watch over my cottage for decades, died a couple of years ago. Since then, it had been standing gray and empty of needles. Its lichen-encrusted branches had added to its ghost like appearance, and kept me wondering how long it might be before this giant might come crashing down to the forest floor, or worse, into my bedroom. Even though the tree was dead, I was reluctant to remove it, knowing such standing snags provide nesting sites for cavity-dwelling birds, such as chickadees, nuthatches, and woodpeckers, which help to control the insect populations.

In my late autumn visit to close the cottage for another season, I found the old black spruce had shed its top fifteen feet – a miniature tree itself with a whorl of branches – hright into the fire pit beside the cedar deck. "Thanks for the early warning," I thought. Best not to leave completion of this task until spring, or I might be presented with a big reconstruction project when I returned.

I'm not a woodsman, just an ex-Boy Scout who still remembers a little about how to fell a tree, where to cut the notches, etc. Without a chain saw, this job would have to done the hard way – with a long handled axe. Sighting up the trunk from all angles, it was hard to tell which direction its mass might favor – maybe north, maybe south. A big difference.

The heft of the heavy axe felt good in my hands. The long wind-up was followed by the satisfying sensation of the blade biting deep into the trunk. The bark fell away easily in big sheaths that had barely been attached, exposing the scars of insect tunnels in the sapwood. The enthusiasm of the first dozen of few swings began to ebb. In the heavy sweatshirt, my body heat soared, and my breath came hard. Progress which seemed so promising after the first few swings, slowed to imperceptible gains, and quite a lot of trunk was left to cut through.

What had I taken on? My body was not in condition for such work, yet I couldn't leave the job to the caprice of the winter storms. I was humbled by the dead old giant who stood stiffly resolute, holding its ground and challenging both my strength and manhood.

How I wished my older son, Hodge, were here to help. Tall and Lincolnesque, an avid rail-splitter and axe man, the two of us could have worked in harmony. I imagined how the sound and rhythm of our alternate blows would echo through the forest, speaking of our connection with one another and the woods, without the angry snarl of the chainsaw breaking the peace of the woods. My other son, Terry, would move in, wordlessly gather the slash to the beach and feed a great fire. There he would remain alone with his private reflections until well into the morning. But this day I would have to be content with the image of their presence.

Then, I recalled an essay written by Aldo Leopold about how he and another sawyer took down a great oak tree that had been killed by lightning. As the saw flew between the two of them, cutting through rings of history, he would call out, "Rest!" every so often. Then, he would relate the events that were going on at the time represented by the rings of the "Good Oak." Mostly these events were milestones in conservation, both good and bad.

"Rest!" Yes indeed, that was what was called for. My task deserved to be slowed, so I, too, could reflect on the antiquity of this tree and all it might have seen. The old spruce should not be disposed of with ease and lack of consideration. It became clear to me that I was meant to be fully present in this work, to become aware of its meaning at a deeper level. God had taken many more decades to grow this tree than he had taken to grow me. In the end, both of us would return to the soil, but hopefully not without some acknowledgement of or history and recognition of our place in the web of life.

I told myself not to be in conflict with the old spruce, not to

C. Kenny-Carter ©

consider it to be an obstacle to be overcome in mindless efforting and anxiousness to get the job over with.

Better to move deliberately, and with reverence. Be present with each swing, sound, and breath. Rest and reflect when tired.

So slowly did the cut advance into the trunk, that I wondered if I could finish before it was time to leave. The chips piled up, the wedge grew deeper and deeper, yet there was no hint of movement. "Which way will you go, Old One," I wondered, "the way I have planned or the way of your own choosing?" I began to consider what I would say to the phone company, to Wisconsin Public Service, and the insurance adjuster. Would I just admit my stupidity at not hiring a professional? No, damn it, this is between the tree and me! It had stood watch so long, with its spear-like shape piercing the night sky above my evening fires. This was my job, my responsibility, however it turned out. Still, I had had enough for the morning and walked away for a time.

Later in the afternoon, I tried an antique logging saw that had been hanging unused in my cabin. What sticky work it turned out to be without another man on the other end to help feed the blade back and forth. The saw blade was rusty and dull. But I was getting closer, and was well under the notch cut on the other side, back to the axe. By now, my arms were shaking, but the trunk remained as upright as ever. In spite of ebbing strength, I was committed to seeing the deed through to the end. Finally, I placed a steel wedge in the high notch at an angle and swung my maul with all I had left. Steel rang on steel, once, twice, three times, followed by a loud cracking sound. The great spruce leaned a bit, and then stopped. Its trunk had been severed, but the tree would not fall. Stubbornly, its upper portion stood with all its weight upon the stump.

Blows to the side of the tree with my maul at last broke it free. The trunk pivoted 45 degrees on its base, and dropped to the ground alongside the stump. Caught in the uplifted arms of a companion cedar

C. Kenney-Carter ©

equal in stature, it still would not fall. Leaning slightly away from the cottage and towards the woods, the ancient spruce was only ten degrees from vertical. Enough! I could do no more! This "woodsman" was headed for the showers and a good nap.

In the pink light of early dawn coming from the lake side, I looked out my bedroom window and saw the old spruce lying in dignified repose, suspended parallel to the ground by its lateral branches. During the night, the great tree had been released from the arms of the cedar and had descended so quietly it didn't awaken me. The spruce had the final say, choosing its own time and direction to descend with dignity, unseen, unheard. Lucky for me, its trajectory was away from where I was sleeping. The big gap that now filled the skyline of large trees reminded me of the missing man formation flown by pilots to honor a fallen comrade. The distinctive spruce spire rising among the rounded cedar tops will always be fixed in my mind when I gaze up at the sky from my deck.

Now I was left with the question of how to handle the "remains." Just leaving the massive tree to slowly sink to the earth, to become soil again would be the easiest solution, but it seemed so wasteful to my pragmatic mind. Surely that inevitable outcome could be forestalled in some useful way. I wished I had the skills to carve a totem pole, but I didn't. Perhaps splitting the long, straight trunk into rails to replace my rotting rustic fence would be a useful way of honoring the tree, keeping the memory of a being who had been such a prominent symbol of my life here at the forest edge. But what did it matter really? Raw wood doesn't last long in this damp area, and nothing lasts forever. I, too, felt the inexorable hand of change on my own body.

So the old spruce was down. Long live the spruce! That night I would have a big ceremonial fire to celebrate our time together in this sacred place. All afternoon I whacked away at the spiral of dead branches. Most were brittle and yielded easily to my axe with a sharp "crack." The pile grew large by sundown. I left the limbs underneath the trunk to support it in its suspension above the ground. I liked the position – a kind of levitation that was arresting to the eye and stimulating to the imagination.

That evening, with the pyramid of neatly stacked limbs ignited by a single match, a fiery tongue split the night sky. It seemed to draw the full harvest moon, in curiosity, from the lake's far horizon. Showers of sparks shot high, as from a giant battery of Fourth of July sparklers. The lichens and pendulous moss on the tree's limbs sizzled in a frenzy of flame, and I felt the passion of the moment rising in my breast. The fire told the whole story: from the wild zest of unrestrained flame to its quiet warmth for comfort and contemplation, to the peace of resolution in its embers, yielding to the cold of the November night, and the end of another season of endless cycles.

C. Kenney-C. ©

last days in door

*O*ne last day in Door County,
　　after flowing like a river.
　　One last sunrise over Lake Michigan,
　　snapping me awake with promise.
　　One last walk up beloved Appleport Road,
　　my shadow striding on stilts twenty feet ahead.
　　One last cinnamon roll at Grandma's Bakery,
　　its memory still kissing my lips.
　　One last pause in front of fall's colors,
　　wishing I could hold them longer.
　　One last look outside my cabin window,
　　watching the lively flight of chickadees.
　　One last fire of cedar splits,
　　holding off the deepening chill.
　　One last stare at the delicious Milky Way,
　　illuminating my humility.
　　One last season slipping into another,
　　before I am ready.
　　One last wish,
　　and I move on.

C. Kenney-C. ©

about the author

A life-long observer of nature, Richard Carter has taken many solitary journeys into the heart of nature and his own in search of deeper connections with the world. He is the author of *Cabin Fever*, a collection of nature essays, with drawings by Carolyn Kenney-Carter. Richard has also published his poetry in several regional literary magazines including, *Rhino, Midway Review, Spoon River Anthology, The Wisconsin Poet's Calendar,* and others. His articles and essays have appeared in *Silent Sports, Warbirds, The Door Voice, The Door Reminder,* and in numerous publications devoted to nature and aviation. His writings have won both the Jade Ring Award and first place in the Al P. Nelson contests of the Wisconsin Regional Writers' Association. Carter has taught nature writing courses at the Redbird Studios in Milwaukee, and at The Clearing in Ellison Bay, as well one-day workshops in a number of locations.

He holds a masters degree in geography from Northwestern University, and after retiring from a 40-year career in city planning, completed additional post-graduate work in environmental studies at Northeastern Illinois University in Chicago. Subsequently, he has been an active volunteer in habitat restoration with a variety of organizations and engaged in aerial photography for The Nature Conservancy and the Fish and Wildlife Service.

Carter currently resides in Wauwatosa, Wisconsin six months of the year and winters in Tucson, Arizona. In both locations, he is engaged in one of his other great passions, the restoration of old airplanes – at the Experimental Aircraft Association in Oshkosh, Wisconsin, and the Pima Air and Space Museum in Tucson, Arizona. Summers he spends as much time as he possibly can in his Door County cabin, where most of his essays for *Through the Cabin Door* were written.

C. Kenney-Carter

about the artist

*C*arolyn Kenney-Carter's drawings and paintings reflect her lifelong connection with the natural world, whether she is depicting scenes or subjects from the wilds or those from her daily life. The near and familiar are what she is drawn to – creatures, things, and places with which she has had a close personal encounter. Even plants or the objects of a still life seem to have emotional content. "We have a relationship," she says. "And when I look deeply, see what's really there, I find new things in what I'm drawing or painting, and in myself." Drawing and watercolor provide the ideal media for her expressive work, which demonstrates strong composition and a high sensitivity for color, light, texture, and detail.

Initially a graphic designer, Kenney-Carter's first venture into fine art came during a session at The Clearing in Door County, Wisconsin, in 1992. There she also met writer, now husband, Richard E. Carter, with whom she created *Cabin Fever*, a book of essays and pencil drawings on the theme of reconnecting with the natural world (Galde Press, 1995, 1998, 2006, 2008, 2010). *Through the Cabin Door* is its sequel. She also did the design and illustration for *Begin With A Seed*, a guide to growing Wisconsin prairie plants (Riveredge Nature Center, 1999), and an ongoing series on native trees of Wisconsin at The Clearing by Executive Director Michael Schneider. Animal subjects are Kenney-Carter's favorites, and her work has been featured in nature specialty shows, on pieces for the University of Wisconsin's School of Veterinary Medicine, on the covers of the *Journal of the American Veterinary Medicine Association*, and in animal portrait commissions.

A graduate of the University of Wisconsin-Madison, and former artist for Milwaukee's natural history and art museums, Kenney-Carter's career path has led to advertising art direction, then a master's degree in business management. She lives and works in Wauwatosa, WI, where in 1986 she began her own creative services firm, WonderCat Graphics (Ace the Wonder Cat, Founder/CEO). Door County, Wisconsin, is one of her prime creative venues, as is Tucson, Arizona, her winter home. In 1996, she began to turn the focus of her business to fine art, as well as design and illustration. Kenney-Carter is a member of the Transparent Watercolor Society of America, the League of Milwaukee Artists, and the Door County Art League, and a signature member of the Southern Arizona Watercolor Guild.

C. Kenney-Carter

artist's notes

Through the Cabin Door (title page)

Title page: Originally used to store commercial fishing equipment, this Door County rustic twine shanty was moved inland to a woodland site on the Larson property.

Acknowledgments

Page xiii: The opossum (*Didelphus virginianus*) is a unique and amazing creature – the only species of the marsupial order in North America. It has a prehensile tail, an opposable big toe, and its young spend several months of their development nursing in their mother's pouch. Its habits are nocturnal and nomadic, and it frequently moves its den – sometimes every night in warmer weather. It is best known for its instinctive habit of feigning death when threatened and unable to escape – "playing possum," as the expression goes.

Introduction

Page xix: The most extensive colonies of large-flowered trillium (*Trillium grandiflora*) grow in beech-maple forests, arising in spring from perennial rhizomes. They are often found in association with clones of trout lily, both species carpeting the woodland floor. For the first six years, trilliums produce only one-leaf and three-leaf forms before blooming for the first time. The spectacular white flowers have three petals, which often turn pink as they age.

Through the Cabin Door (poem)

Page 1: The branches of the arborvitae, or northern white-cedar (*Thuja occidentalis*) come out of the trunk at right angles. But in mature trees, they often curve gracefully downward in the middle, then up at the top. This is especially true where light is limited, or the tree is rooted in a precarious spot. The arborvitae branches experience a seasonal needle drop in fall, rather than shedding their old foliage gradually, like most evergreens. The two- to five-year-old needles turn yellow, then brown and drop. The remaining needles fade until spring.

Page 5: This white-footed, or deer mouse *(Peromyscus leucopus* or *Peromyscus maniculatus)* is one of a series who have nested in the drawer of the seed table on the deck of "The Word Shop." The spot provides both warmth and protection, and ready access to food. Typically, they have litters of three to five young – tiny, pink, and transparent at birth, but weaned, furred, and mobile by three to four weeks. (These two species are similar and hard to tell apart, so their names are often combined as "white-footed deer mouse.")

Opening a New Season

Page 7: Paper birch trunks *(Betula papyrifera)* along South Appleport Lane display the frayed and curled bark layers that peel away along the lines of lenticels – the openings that let air into the tree trunk. This boreal forest species has six to nine layers of white bark, which reflect the sun and prevent premature warming on sunny winter days.

Page 11: Canada geese *(Branta canadensis)* come in to land over the Lake Michigan shoreline, a smaller subflock made up of family units. Most arrive at their breeding ranges by earliest spring, returning to their nesting site from the year before. The yearling geese soon leave for other sites, usually to the north, and may bond as pairs, but seldom breed until their second or third season. As the snow and ice begin to melt, the mature Canada geese are among the first species to nest and aggressively defend territory.

Page 13: Bold and boisterous black-capped chickadees *(Poecile atricapilla)* feed at the seed table behind "The Word Shop." Outside of the breeding season, they are often seen in small groups that move continuously through the woodland. Within these flocks, they display complex interactions and vocalizations to communicate and establish dominance.

Page 15: The red squirrel *(Tamiasciurus hudsonicus)*, lounging on the cedar branches behind "The Word Shop," is usually one of the feistiest creatures in the northern woods. Unlike gray squirrels, whose ranges overlap, red squirrels are intensely territorial, and typically chase each other, and even birds, away from food sources. Each has defined paths through the trees in their defended space, and will scamper up the nearest trunk, wave its tail, chatter and scold at any intruder from above.

In Search of Appleport

Page 19: Hover Torgeson's rustic cabin at the intersection of Appleport Road and South Appleport Lane dates back to about 1914. At one point, when a fire had destroyed the nearby Larson home, the entire family moved into this cottage until their home could be rebuilt. Uninhabited in more recent times, the roof has sagged and begun to fall in, and the walls continue to deteriorate with each passing year.

Page 23: This antique gear wheel is from machinery once used to wind up fishing nets, found in Door County, Wisconsin, in one of the rustic structures on the Larson property off Appleport Road.

Page 25: This restored Door County log cabin off Old Stage Road was built for the sawyers who originally cleared the trees on the land nearby.

Page 29: This Door County fishing boat and these net floats are moored at Sand Bay, between Baileys Harbor and Rowleys Bay, Wisconsin, on the Lake Michigan side of the Door County Peninsula.

Page 31: White-cedars, or arborvitae *(Thuja occidentalis)* and a great blue heron *(Ardia heroias)* who fishes in the shallows are common along the Appleport beach shoreline along Lake Michigan. The white-cedar grows in both cold, alkaline swamps and dry limestone soils, which may argue in favor of two genetic strains. In any case, correct soil pH seems more important than moisture content. Its sprawling root system is adapted to cope with either shallow soil levels or excess water. Trunks are often lobed or buttressed at the base, often leaning or twisting.

Chomp, Chomp

Page 35: The porcupine *(Erethizon dorsatum)* has small eyes and poor vision, seeing well only very close up, especially at night when it is most active. However, its sense of smell is excellent, useful in its extensive and solitary wanderings, as it is non-territorial.

Page 39: Porcupine *(Erethizon dorsatum)* feed on the tender inner (cambium) bark layer of both evergreens and hardwoods. They also browse on swollen spring buds, especially of maples; the acorns of oaks; and the small cones of hemlocks, nipping off the tips of branches, stripping them, and then dropping the twigs on the ground.

Page 43: The porcupine *(Erethizon dorsatum)* is said to have a taste for salt, and often chews anything with a human sweat residue, such as ax and shovel handles, shed doors and windows, and outhouse seats. The glue in fiberboard and plywood is likewise a treat.

Page 45: "Mama Coon" and three of her juvenile offspring feed at the seed table behind "The Wood Shop" cabin. The raccoon *(Procyon lotor)* typically has litters of three to five young, who join her to forage for food at the age of about ten weeks. They become independent at four to five months, but will stay within their mother's range throughout their first year.

Raccoons are "omnivores," which is to say that they will eat almost anything – fruit, berries, and vegetables; frogs, crayfish, and insects; birdseed, nuts; and food scraps or garbage. They are most active at night, the particulars depending upon the availability of food, the season and the weather, the sex of the animal, and whether it has dependent offspring with it.

Slaughter of the Elders

Page 49: Arborvitae or northern white-cedar trunks *(Thuja occidentalis)* twist to the light, as their roots cling to the sparse, rocky soil.

Page 53: These damaged tree remnants are all that remained of the white-cedar stand that was cut for lumber off South Appleport Lane, Door County, Wisconsin.

Page 55: A gape-mouthed cedar stump stands in shock amidst the wreckage of part of the forest off South Appleport Lane, Door County, Wisconsin.

Page 59: The yellow lady's slipper *(Cyripedium calceolus)* is found in two species forms in Door County, Wisconsin. The large yellow lady's slipper grows in woodlands, and is one to two feet high, with a flower over an inch long with yellow-green, twisted petals. The small yellow lady's slipper grows in more damp soil, such as boggy spots, hollows, and roadside ditches, and has a smaller flower with purple petals.

In and Out of Time

Page 63: Curving out over a dolomite ledge, and arborvitae, or northern white-cedar *(Thuja occidentalis)* clings to a cliff overlooking Green Bay at The

Clearing, Ellison Bay, Wisconsin. In spite of the severe growing conditions on the Niagara Escarpment – thin soil, with limited moisture and nutrients, and harsh, dry winds – the arborvitae survives.

Page 67: Richard Carter's yellow seagoing kayak, a.k.a. as "The Banana Boat," rests, awaiting new adventures near the old fishing dock at the Appleport beach. The original dock dates back to the early 1900s, but was partially refurbished in the 1990s.

Page 69: Jens Jensen's Cliff House cabin at The Clearing, Ellison Bay, Wisconsin, can be seen in part from the waters of Green Bay behind the screen of white-cedars that covers the cliff face.

Page 71: Jens Jensen's Cliff House cabin at The Clearing, Ellison Bay, Wisconsin, is seen from the steep natural steps leading down from the hiking path along the cliffs above Green Bay. This was Jensen's hidden spot for rest and personal reflection, away from the rest of The Clearing.

Turkey Trot

Page 75: The wild turkey hen (*Meleagris gallopavo*) is always on the alert for predators, especially when she has her poults nearby. The horn of fleshy tissue on top of her beak becomes enlarged when she is alarmed by potential danger.

Page 79: The stump and roots of a giant arborvitae, or northern white-cedar root (*Thuja occidentalis*) sit in a patch of thimbleberry bushes in an open woodland off Robin Lane.

Page 81: The wild turkey hen (*Meleagris gallopavo*), "strutting her stuff," seeks to draw attention away from our poults, who feed on the ground with her. Heavy-bodied, wild turkeys prefer to avoid danger by running, though they roost in trees at night.

Page 83: A wild turkey hen and her poults (*Meleagris gallopavo*) feed in open woodlands or forest clearings on insects, acorns, fruit, and seeds. The poults initially roost beneath their mother's wings for several weeks, as they are most at risk from cold and/or rain. After a month, the young birds begin to roost in trees.

Creating Community

Page 85: This room number plaque (designed by Erik Rinkleff) and traditional Adirondack chair at a student dormitory were fashioned by Work Week volunteers at The Clearing, Ellison Bay, Wisconsin. The native vine, Virginia creeper *(Parthenocissus quinquefolia)* sprawls over the wall.

Page 89: Jens Jensen's original entrance road to The Clearing, Ellison Bay, Wisconsin, makes gentle, sweeping curves through maple, beech, birch, hemlock, and mixed evergreen woods, slowing down the driver to a peaceful pace.

Page 91: Richard Carter removes screens and washes windows on the Main Lodge at The Clearing, Ellison Bay, Wisconsin – one of the major tasks there handled by Work Week volunteers.

Skiing Newport State Park

Page 95: White-tailed deer *(Odocoileus virginianus)* make deep tracks, as they break through deep or crusted late winter snows. They may leave large holes, nine to twelve feet apart, where all feet land in the same spot. They may also gather in yards or create packed paths, or deer runs, which are used by many deer to travel and locate food with greater ease in severe weather.

Page 99: Richard Carter heads down the cross-country ski trails through cedar and hemlock stands at Newport Beach Park, Door County, Wisconsin, near the Mink River outlet, leading to primitive camping sites.

Page 101: Meadow voles *(Microtus pennsylvanicus)* create neat tunnels through grassy areas by biting off the plant growth on the sides and bottom of the path. In winter, when the snow is four inches or more deep, the voles will tunnel through the snow, creating winding paths through fields and open woodlands. These paths can most often be seen as the surface snow begins to melt.

Too Early in Spring Woods

Page 103: Bloodroot *(Sanguinaria canadensis)* is one of the first spring ephemeral wildflowers to bloom, and an indicator of moist, humus-rich woods throughout Wisconsin. Its showy white flowers are self-pollinating, and appear only briefly, while the single lobed leaf that partially clasps each stem persists longer.

Page 107: A sandhill crane *(Grus canadensis)* makes a stopover at a cornfield to feed on waste grain during its early spring journey back north. A bird of open marshes and grasslands, sandhills breed in scattered pairs, but gather in flocks, which are often large and noisy, for migration.

Going to Grandma's

Page 109: A herring gull *(Larus argentatus)* sits among broken slabs of dolomite along the Green Bay shoreline. This is the most widespread of the large gull species, and variations in its size, structure, and plumage make it hard to identify with complete certainty.

Page 113: A solitary male common goldeneye drake *(Bucephala clangula)* swims along the shoreline near the Rowleys Bay Resort (formerly the Wagon Trail Resort), Door County, Wisconsin, patrolling its fixed territory of a nest site and the surrounding area where it will feed and preen. Among the earliest spring migrants, goldeneyes begin to arrive on their defended spaces as soon as open water appears. In winter, they are more commonly seen in small flocks.

Page 115: Cinnamon rolls and pecan rolls – voted "Best in Wisconsin" – and coffee at Grandma's Bakery, the Rowleys Bay Resort, are always a special treat, as are some of the distinctive features seen through the window – the old schoolhouse bell, the waterfront cross, and the waterfront and forested shore beyond it.

Sailing on the Silurian Sea

Page 117: Typically, the eastern gray tree frog *(Hyla versicolor)* sings in midsummer in woodlands near water. This one came regularly to sun himself on the deck of the Appleport cottage one season, often sitting on one of the chunks of Silurian coral collected from the old beach ridges on the property. Chain, horn, and brain corals are shown here.

Page 121: Mixed vegetation and rough steps of dolomite fragments lead up the old beach ridge on which Richard Carter built his cabin – "The Word Shop."

Page 125: The rocky beach below the Green Bay cliffs at The Clearing, Ellison Bay, Wisconsin, is littered with chunks of dolomite which have broken away from the layered face of the shoreline, as well as rounded stones smoothed by the water.

Page 127: Arborvitae, or northern white-cedar *(Thuja occidentalis)* mature slowly under the often harsh conditions of the boreal forest, and so have thin, dense layers of growth. This giant cedar root, resting among rounded beach rocks on the Appleport beach, has endured many years of weathering there.

The Joys of Restoration

Page 131: Distinguished by its rattling call, the belted kingfisher *(Megaceryle alcyon)* flies as much as 20 feet above its stream or shoreline territory. Spotting a small fish, it dives headlong, captures its prey, then lands on a perch and beats it against the branch before tossing it in the air and swallowing its meal headfirst.

Page 135: Painted turtles *(Chrysemys picta),* shown basking on a log along Sawyer Creek Savanna, Oshkosh, Wisconsin, are probably the most common and widespread of turtle species. Often these small (5–6") turtles are seen in groups, sunning on logs or rocks in ponds, swamps, ditches, or slow-moving rivers and streams.

Page 139: A gray squirrel *(Sciurus carolinensis)* feeds along a path through bur oak and shagbark hickory trees in the Sawyer Creek Savanna. The fruit of both of these dominant trees provides an abundance of food and shelter for squirrels and other wildlife year-round.

Page 141: The muskrat *(Ondatra zibethicus)* is found in a wide range of habitats, from the country to urban sites. Wherever water and cattails or bulrushes are found, muskrats are apt to be seen. Often mistaken for beavers, they are actually only 1/10 to 1/4 that size, and have thin tails that trail visibly or are held up when they swim, whereas beavers have broad, flat tails which they carry underwater.

Mourning the Dove

Page 143: The mourning dove *(Zenaida macroura)* sits on its nest, which is a loose construction of twigs. It nests singly, but feeds in small flocks on the ground.

Page 147: The mourning dove *(Zenaida macroura)* is the smallest of the northern doves and distinguished by its slender and long tapered tail, as well as the whistling sound made by its wings.

End of a Season

Page 149: The yellow-bellied sapsucker *(Sphyrapicus varius)* is widespread in the northern forest in summer. While quiet and retiring, they can be seen drilling parallel rows of small holes around live tree trunks, notably in basswood. Later, they return to feed on the oozing sap and small insects.

Page 153: The black spruce *(Picea mariana)* is the characteristic tree of boreal wetlands. A flat, shallow root system makes it possible for this species to grow in the thin soils of northern bogs, but also makes it subject to being blown over by strong, northern winds. Propped up on its branches, this fallen black spruce at the Appleport cottage appears suspended in midair.

Page 155: Northern white-cedar, or arborvitae *(Thuja occidentalis)*, grows more slowly, even under the most ideal conditions. Just an inch of trunk diameter may take ten to twenty years to develop. Thin bark makes this species vulnerable to fire, and it may suffer browning and death of branches from thaws in late winter or early spring. When the leaves lose large amounts of water, they cannot replace the moisture from their still-frozen roots. The broken top of a white-cedar tree at Appleport cottage may have been weakened in one or more of these ways, and so snapped off in the wind.

Last Days in Door

Page 159: Rich blue-purple fringed gentians *(Gentiana crinita)* bloom in wet meadows, damp woods, and stream banks in late summer and fall, along the Mink River Estuary in northern Door County, Wisconsin, for example. Unlike most other wildflowers, which are perennials, fringed gentians are annuals, and reproduce through fine, wind-scattered seed.

About the Author

Page 163: Trout lilies with yellow or white flowers (*Erythronium americanum* and *Erythronium albidum*) grow in widespread, interconnected clones across the forest floor in early spring. They are also called adder's tongue, or fawn lilies because of the dappled pattern on their leaves. The individual plantlets do not bloom until the year they develop a pair of leaves, instead of a single one.

About the Artist

Page 167: The eastern chipmunk (*Tamias striatus*) is active during the day, and spends most of its time foraging to fill its cheek pouches and carry its finds to build up its food supply in its burrow. Here is the center of its life, where it will alternate gathering with periods of rest, seek protection from predators, and sleep during the winter. A skilled architect, chipmunks will often build an elaborate complex of tunnels, with the entrance at a substantial distance from the main chambers.

Artist's Notes

Page 171: The pink and white showy lady's slippers (*Cyripedium reginae*) bloom in wetter habitats – swamps, bogs, and roadside hollows, typically in late June at The Ridges Sanctuary, Baileys Harbor, Wisconsin.